ॐ

‖‖ ‖ ‖‖‖‖‖‖‖‖‖‖ ‖‖‖ ‖‖ ‖‖
I0134522

Aloha, Mr. Hand: An Alternative Trip through Education
Published by Overhead Projections, LLC
Castle Pines

Library of Congress Control Number: 2016909946
Klinkerman, Anthonette, Author
Aloha, Mr. Hand: An Alternative Trip through Education
Anthonette Klinkerman

ISBN: 978-0-9905999-1-3

EDUCATION/Alternative

QUANTITY PURCHASES: Schools, companies, professional groups, clubs, and other organizations may qualify for special terms when ordering quantities of this title. For information, email admin@overheadprojections.net.

ഓരു

This book is dedicated to all of my Eaglets for allowing me to spend some time with you on your educational journey. It was a privilege denied to many,
and I count myself lucky to have known you.

Also dedicated to Doug Seligman, to the teachers who soldier on in those halls, and to educators everywhere who may have wondered at some point in their career,
What ever happened to that kid?

Prologue:

This is not a "How-To Teach Alternative Education" book. If that is what you were expecting, you are going to be sorely disappointed. There isn't an answer to that question no matter where you look, or what "expert" you consult. For that matter, there isn't a How-To book on regular teaching either. Teaching is something one must experience, and then it becomes an either/or proposition. Either you love it, or you don't. You're either cut out for it, or you aren't. There is no going half-heartedly into this profession. Over time you'll get stronger, or you'll quit. The tired fact that many new teachers don't make it past year five is still true. Teaching is fluid; ever-changing, dynamic, and constantly evolving. (And this is without all the political nonsense thrown in on top.) I have been at this for a total of 17 years, and I am still trying to figure out what I am going to do next. It makes me feel like I owe former students an apology for some of my early teaching, but I certainly will not apologize for caring about each and every one of them to the very core of their being.

So this book will not have answers. It will have a lot of stories, some nuggets of truth, plenty of tales from the heart, and the painful baring of souls, mostly mine. Read it in order, or skip around; it's all up to you.

One last thing: buckle up. This is going to get, to borrow a phrase, gnarly.

I stumbled across this journal entry after a full day of working on this book as if the fates intended:

08/22/2005

My First Day as a Teacher at Eagle

Wow! What a night! What a feeling, to be back in the classroom after my daughter was born. To be honest, I'd only been out a year as my ACC (Arapahoe Community College) job once a week kept me in tune. But back with high school students: there really is a difference between them and college students. I don't know what it is – can't put

소(cr)

my finger on it. Perhaps it's the choice of wanting to be there versus having to be there? I think that may be it. Because really, with my ACC students, there's only a one-year difference [in age].

Little did I know then the key to education, in all its forms, is the making-kids-want-to-be-there part.

ଽୠଔ

Layout:

Throughout the book, readers will find sections titled "In Their Own Words"*. These are former students, and their parents, perhaps even teachers, who graciously agreed to contribute their stories and perspectives and allowed me to use their names. Their stories are real, raw, beautiful, heart-breaking, and everything in between. To be sure, I owe all of them a debt of gratitude for opening up their lives to me, and being willing to share their stories with those not fortunate enough to have been one of their teachers.

A reader will also find "Graduation Write-ups". I took it upon myself to do a little "citizen journalism" and contribute reports of the graduation ceremonies held twice a year to the YourHub.com section of *The Denver Post*. Graduation is considered a June event, and therefore forgotten when it is done in any other form. These kids deserved their moment in the limelight along with all the other graduates mentioned in local papers, so I gave it to them.

Disclaimer: As red pen-trigger-happy English teacher with Grammar Ninja-like reflexes, I reserved the right to edit entries for clarity, though attempting to stay true to the writer's voice. However, feel free to keep believing that I cured all my writers of grammatical errors forever.

ಹೃಾಡ

<u>Introduction and Some Answers</u>

So who, exactly, is an alternative/ "at-risk" kid? Before I try to provide some kind of insight to that question, I have to point out the futility of labeling people. We tell our students constantly not to stereotype, not to label, and yet in education we are the worst offenders. Years ago I had a student who was brilliant at math but couldn't write his own name. His parent introduced me to the term *Twice-Exceptional*. And then I didn't hear it again. As it happens, 15 years later I attended a training regarding and titled "The Twice-Exceptional Child". The descriptions of multiple categories of this type of learner were presented, and like a dance-floor strobe light, there was a column denoting the "At-risk" student. It struck me that this may very well be the explanation people seek when defining what makes alternative education a better fit for a certain population.

A Twice-Exceptional child, like anyone, has his or her strengths in one area, and his or her weaknesses in another, and often the two mask each other. In summary, there are about six different types of Twice Exceptional child, but for all intents and purposes, I am going to focus on just the one, the "At-risk".

When I first heard the term "at-risk", I thought *Of what? Failure? Dropping out? Drug-use? All of the above?* That is partially correct, though I never liked the term as it seemed so damning. So defeatist. But it was the only label around at the time for these types of kids.

Often, I would encounter a student who would perform in a stellar manner in my classroom. There should have been no reason for them to wind up in an alternative education setting, but there they were. I eventually figured out they were that population of student who were "Brilliant but Bored". (If you're like every other acronym-loving educator out there, use "3B".) In this training, however, the column titled "At-risk" (See Figure A below) jumped out at me like a neon sign. The pieces of the puzzle that is an alternative education student somewhat fell into place. At-risk kids seem to be Twice-Exceptional kids when no one yet had that label, but I am not still 100% convinced they should be placed entirely in this "box".

Characteristics of the At-risk Twice-Exceptional child:

Feelings and Attitudes	Behaviors	Needs	Adult/Peer Perceptions	Identification
Resentful and angry Depressed Reckless & manipulative Poor self-concept Defensive Unrealistic expectations Unaccepted Resistive to authority Not motivated by teacher-driven rewards A subgroup is anti-social	Creates crises and causes disruptions Thrill-seeking Will work for the relationship Intermittent attendance Pursues outside interests Low academic achievement May be self-isolating Often creative Criticizes self and others Produces inconsistent work	Safety and structure An "alternative" environment An individualized program Confrontation and accountability Alternatives (in assignments) Professional counseling Direction and short term goals	Adults may be angry with them Peers are judgmental Seen as troubled or irresponsible Seen as rebellious May be afraid of them May be afraid for them Adults feel powerless to help them	Individual IQ testing Achievement subtests Interviews Auditions Nonverbal measures of intelligence Parent nominations Teacher nominations

Figure A: Maureen Neihart and George Betts, 2010

Check here, check there, check that one, and check that one.

The funny thing about my educational past was I went to the private, college-preparatory high school, Francis W. Parker, in San Diego, literally across the street from an alternative education school known as Mark Twain. That was where "the bad kids" went while my classmates and I studied our hearts out for our very certain collegiate futures.

Cue the "foreshadowing" music

That little black sign was the only indication of a school within a school.

Setting the Scene

Raucous voices and blaring music greeted me as I stepped out into the hall to keep an eye on passing period after a particularly grueling second period class. My neighboring teacher asked, "Everything okay?"

"Sure," I said. "Just that one kid, XYZ…He totally reminds me of Jeff Spicoli."

"I don't have him," said this much younger new teacher.

Incredulous that he wasn't getting my 80s pop culture allusion, I said, "Please tell me you're kidding."

"I don't have him," he insisted.

It was that very moment I knew I was getting close to passing the "Seasoned" teacher mark. One night over dinner, this young teacher had admitted being born the year I graduated from high school in 1986. Of course he wouldn't get a *Fast Times at Ridgemont High* reference.

Nine years earlier, I entered the high school from an obscure side door on a summer afternoon, climbed the stairs as directed, and turned right. I moved down the hall, and found my interview team of two waiting for me in a windowless room, seated at a conference table situated under exposed heating vents, surrounded by file cabinets, a refrigerator, and a microwave on a shelf.

Settling into an aged chair, I couldn't stop myself and blurted, "I didn't even know you were here!" What I meant was I had no idea that there was a school within a school, an alternative night high school housed within a cavernous high school in Douglas County, Colorado. The principal stated, "We are the stealth school of the district. The problems it doesn't want to admit we have. Teen pregnancy, drug abuse, truancy, etc." It was a one-year position for a woman on maternity leave, and I had just spent a year at home with my own baby and was ready to go back to work. I took the two-nights-a-week job.

The staff lounge/workroom/meeting room/storage/dining area. I was interviewed here, and ate many dinners under those vents, but today it is the student store.

There are a few Hollywood movies about troubled kids in the classrooms of struggling schools, but allow me to remind some of you more seasoned folks of the 1970s situation comedy, *Welcome Back,*

9

Kotter. John Travolta found some early success here, if you recall. According to Wikipedia, "the show stars stand-up comedian and actor Gabriel 'Gabe' Kaplan as the title character, Gabe Kotter, a wisecracking teacher who returns to his alma mater, James Buchanan High School in Brooklyn, New York, to teach a remedial class of loafers, called 'Sweathogs.' Befitting its low ranking, Kotter's class is held in Room 111. The school's principal is referred to, but rarely seen on-screen. The rigid vice principal, Michael Woodman, dismisses the Sweathogs as witless hoodlums, and only expects Kotter to contain them until they drop out or are otherwise banished. As a former remedial student, and a founding member of the original class of Sweathogs, Kotter befriends the current Sweathogs and stimulates their potential. A pupil-teacher rapport is formed, and the students often visit Kotter's Bensonhurst apartment, sometimes via the fire-escape window, much to the chagrin of his wife, Julie."

Sounds very, very familiar, minus the fire-escape.

Chapter One - Ignition

"Begin at the beginning," the King said, very gravely, "and go on till you come to the end: then stop."
— Lewis Carroll, Alice in Wonderland

It was never my intention to become an alternative education teacher. I was going to be a private school education teacher, my kids in neat rows and sporting crisp uniforms. What I thought was going to be a nice little detour, teaching one night-time Creative Writing class from 7:15 – 9:00, became a ten-year stint in an alternative education high school in one of the wealthiest districts in America.

My total experience in public education comes to 17 years. I did my student teaching in elementary, middle, and high school, driven by the notion I wanted to be my 10th Grade English teacher when I grew up. The part I had failed to factor in was my high school experience, and the only one I had to go on, was at one of the finest private high schools in San Diego county. Reality smacked me in the face after I did my final student teaching at Madison High School. A quiet student in my class who always sported a black trench coat, strange for sunny Southern California and long before Columbine, disappeared from my class roster one day. I was informed later he had been arrested for the machete he had under that coat. He had brandished it after one too many bullying incidents on the public bus he took to and from school.

There went my image of kids in uniforms and sitting up straight in neat rows. This was before metal detectors became the norm, but it was enough to send me back to the corporate world for a bit as an administrative assistant in an advertising agency. I found after eight months that color-coding files and wrangling sales people in the field wasn't my thing, and I returned to a school district in one of the lesser-known cities in San Diego County. Santee, or "Santucky", as national talk show host Jim Rome calls it. It was a notoriously backwards school district 22 miles inland from the coast, far from the touristy parts of San Diego. Apartments, trailer parks, and horse property surrounded the

ℬↂℛ

enclave. The Klan, yes, that one with a K, met in the high school gym up until 1991. This was now 1997, and I took a job as a "guest teacher", a politically correct term for a substitute, in Santee School District. I substituted every grade level there is from Kindergarten to 8th grade, actually, as this was a K-8 district only. It didn't matter if it was a First grade classroom or a Special Education classroom –substitutes get it all.

One Second grade classroom, I was sitting in the rocking chair for Story Time when I felt a number of little hands on my shoulders, and the little hands started massaging. "What are you doing?" I asked, trying to keep the surprise from my voice.

"Oh, our teacher loves it when we do this," came the reply.

Uh, the understood *No Touching* policy between Teacher and Student was apparently not as clear as I thought.

I said, "That's very nice, but you can sit down and listen to the story."

The kids shrugged and sat back down.

Another day found me in the Special Ed classroom, and I threw the *No Touching* policy out the window when a student was clearly becoming a danger to himself and others. He was in an out-of-control rage, and for whatever instinctive reason I threw my arms around him from behind to capture his own flailing arms. I will never forget feeling him physically relax. At that precise moment I learned that students often are testing to see where the boundaries are, and if anyone cares enough to stop them.

There was another lower grade level teacher who regularly called upon me to substitute as she needed frequent visits to doctor's offices. Without fail she would leave dismal substitute plans, often stating simply to take the kids out for extended recess. I couldn't believe how little actual learning seemed to be going on in this classroom on these many days, and though I scrambled to make some learning happen, I had had enough. I went to the principal one afternoon to express my concern over these so-called plans that a) didn't make her look good and b) made me look bad. Later when this teacher got wind that I had reported what was going on, she confronted me and hissed, "We real teachers don't do that to one another. We support each other."

"Well, you're not going to make me look bad in the process," I replied.

She never again asked me to sub for her, which was a-okay by me.

A Fourth grade classroom taught me very quickly that I would never EVER teach at that grade level. The drama for girl students starts around then, and the teacher was inadvertently fueling it with a Complaint Book. I'm sure this was a good idea at one point – to have students write down their grievances to be discussed later, but it was backfiring in a HUGE way. All day long, for multiple days when I was there, girls would approach with their chins in the air and declare, "I need The Book." All studies would stop as they settled in to write their complaints with their friends hovering about them to make sure they got all the details right.

No, thank you.

I had my heart set on high school. My longest student teaching assignment was in a high school in San Diego County under the guidance of a Master Teacher who had led many a young teacher before me through the process. One afternoon my class had gotten the better of me, and I was left in tears at the end of the day. The Master Teacher came up to me and said, "You just had your first heartbreak as a teacher. You were expecting them to sit there hanging on your every word, and they burst your image of what it was going to be like."

He was right.

Nothing, but nothing will ever prepare you for your first real classroom. Your first year will beat you up and stomp all over your visions of what it was going to be like to be a teacher. It's not a wonder why most beginning teachers do not make it past their first five years – a well-documented fact. Students don't behave like their textbook models, and they could care less about your fabulous bulletin boards. (I really took a certification class where we spent a week on designing bulletin boards.) Mr. Keating from *Dead Poets Society* was fiction. The Freedom Writers Diary only happened because all the planets and stars in the heavens were perfectly aligned.

My first salaried year looked more like I was the next warm body that came along. I was given four Eighth grade English classes, a Sixth grade art class, a Science class, and a Yearbook class. Where was my Prep period? I didn't have one. No teacher did. I was qualified to teach only those English classes, but apparently the State of California didn't so much mind those pesky requirements of a teacher actually knowing their subject back then. Ironically, one of my students went on to win the County Science Fair. It was certainly not from my doing as my science lessons consisted of reading the textbook and watching videos. A LOT of videos.

I was given the art class because I could draw, and Yearbook only because I had some experience from my own high school days. All of this went down in my oddly angled room. We were in a round building because the trend then was to be able to open partitions between the rooms in order to facilitate more community learning. Rarely, if ever, did we open these accordion-esque plastic "drapes"; we were all too busy struggling to maintain discipline over our charges.

Living on in infamy is the story of one of my classes and a video showing I had left for the substitute. I forgot to mention in my plans to leave the light ON, and it was rumored later a male student "found his thrill on Blueberry Hill" at the hands of a promiscuous female student during said video.

We were surrounded by trailer parks and low rent apartments, and never was that more evident than during parent-teacher interactions. There was the time a mom showed up for conferences barefoot, in cutoffs, and quite drunk. Another time a parent burst into the room to berate me about my teaching *as* I was conducting class. Still another time I found one waiting for me to leave my room so she could scream at me in the commons area about saying something about her child after she pulled him from the school. All I had said was, "He may be back here before it's all said and done." Then there was the day even a sheriff's deputy, the principal, AND the student's mother could not get a belligerent sixth grader back in the classroom. I had caught the mother's eye and apparently made a face to the effect of "Wow! This is unreal!", but she then exercised the only control she obviously had and complained to my principal about me.

I wasn't perfect as a new teacher (I'm still not), and by no means am I claiming to be. I learned very quickly to watch what I said and how I said it. But the aforementioned situations, again, we were never taught to cope with in teacher school. There aren't enough classes to cover over three-quarters of the reality one experiences as a teacher. Now that I look back, it's a wonder I didn't become a statistic and quit that first year.

ഏറോ

Chapter Two – And So It Starts…

"Teaching in middle school is like teaching in dog years."
~ A. Klinkerman

My teacher husband and I moved to Colorado in 2000. We had come to visit his family for our one-year anniversary, and ended up moving two weeks later. The school district we both now teach in was expanding exponentially back then, and teachers were desperately needed. We had gone to check out the hiring situation at the district building, even though we were in vacation clothes, and behind the reception desk was the lady to whom my husband had sold his car about ten years before. She knew of an opening at an elementary school and called them sending us up there immediately. The principal was waiting for us, eagerly rubbing her hands together. She hired my husband on the spot, warning him though that he would be the "only rooster in the hen house". Even the janitor was female. She looked at me then and asked me where I wanted to go, and I told her I had just dropped off my resume at the middle school. "I'll call them right now," she said, and that was that. The middle school called when we arrived back in San Diego a few days later and hired me over the phone. Two weeks later we moved into the house we had waiting for us, and two days later started teaching.

I spent one year in the first middle school, then moved to help open another brand new middle school closer to my home. I spent two years there, started my Master's degree program with my husband, and had a little girl in the middle of it. I took a year off to be with my newborn, which then turned into two. By the middle of that second year, my brain was oozing out of my ear from too many *Dora* and *Barney* episodes, and upon my husband's suggestion I found a one-night-a-week community college position teaching a reading skills class. Around this time, I also found the .2 position at the night high school. Over the years I added a class here and there until nine years later I was finally full-time.

The night school hall/day school Foreign Language wing.

My first class was third period Creative Writing, from 7:15 – 9:00. I had about nine students on my roster, and that first night a young lady came in and immediately kicked her feet up on the desk and glared at me. Now there are some fast thinkers in the world, but none quite as fast as a teacher. I knew that if I came down on her for the placement of her feet, the battle would be lost right there. I opted not to say a word, knowing she was daring me to make an issue of it so she could draw out the fight. I also knew she would get uncomfortable eventually, and indeed after some time she shifted her position and was ready to play class. Not a single drop of blood spilled.

I had another student in that class who looked like a refugee from the heavy metal band, Metallica. One night he jumped up from his desk like a fire had been lit beneath him. "Oh, shit! Oh, shit!" he cried. "I had a court date!" He tore from the classroom, an astonished silence hanging in the air for a split second before the peals of laughter broke out from the other students. I couldn't help myself and said, "I honestly don't think I can follow that."

Yes, I'm sarcastic. IN THE CLASSROOM. I know, I know, you are not supposed to be, but let me tell you this – that's the only thing that will save you some days. Younger students do not get sarcasm, I understand, which is why I never thought my being an elementary school teacher was a good idea. Those people hold a special place in heaven, as I am sure they also feel about me. With the older students, especially alternative education students, you can mostly get away with it. I am convinced the people who tell you "You can't use sarcasm in the classroom" have never actually BEEN in a classroom, and therefore can take a long walk off a short pier. See what I did there?

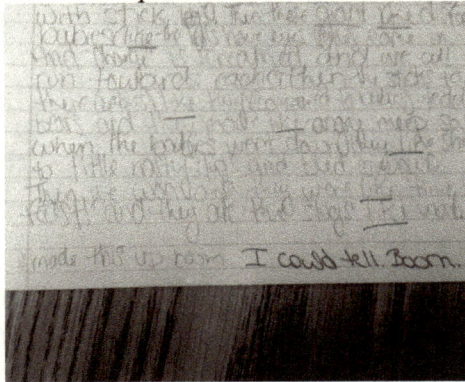

The student wrote: "Made this up. boom." Yes, I am THAT teacher.

If you don't laugh in the classroom, you will cry. Believe me. When you get students from abusive homes, or reading at a third grade level though they are in high school, or their brother ran away the night before, or they are struggling to stay sober or to stop cutting themselves, there has to be some levity somewhere. Laughter is about the only thing that can save you when faced with the students the rest of society has cast off as hopeless. Mind you, this is laughing WITH them, not AT them.

On that note, however, I am a firm believer that a little public humiliation goes a long way. The early American colonists had the right idea with locking the town problem in the stocks for a few days. For that reason, when a kid dropped an F-bomb in my room and had to stand there with my little robotic "Grandma" singing her heart out. She was a gift when I wrote my children's book, and she sings, "Don't you wish your Grandma was hot like me?" all the while dressed in a frock that reads, "They call it Menopause because Mad Cow Disease was taken."

Hey, it worked and kids knew not to cuss in my room. Ever. I even had students from other classes come to get Grandma because someone in another room cussed.

I established a "No profanity" rule in my room at the beginning of each quarter, and if a student slipped up, he or she owed me push-ups or a "dance with Grandma." Before anyone comes unglued and reports me to the authorities, this was NOT capital punishment as it was a <u>choice</u>. And, by the way, it happens plenty in youth sports programs. Most would opt to do the push-ups because the song is so heinous, and so long, and because the rest of the class begged them not to press "Play". How convenient to also effectively remind the rest of the class to watch their language.

I highly recommend the next time you are at a garage sale and find a singing fish plaque or Alvin the Chipmunk, spend a few bucks for a profanity-free high school classroom.

In Their Own Words:

My Eagle story all started when I was a senior at [High School], I had no chance of graduating in 2014 and as the school year came to a close I had a meeting with my counselor, [Named], and she failed to mention Eagle Academy to me earlier in the year which pissed me off to no end. So the summer came around and I went to [High School] and signed the withdrawal papers. I am so happy to say that was the greatest day of my educational career, it was like my final F-you to [High School], the second I stepped into those doors I felt like I was finally home. Eagle has done for me something [High School] never did, Eagle gave me a second chance at getting my diploma, I was finally able to walk across that stage and get my High School diploma.

When I first started I was nervous about the teachers, but when I had first period with Dr. Andrea Rietsch (or mama Rietsch) all my nerves just washed away, the amount and love and support she has for her "babies", was so uplifting and I was actually excited to come to school. As for the students I gained a tighter close knit family here than I ever did back at [High School]. The students from Eagle didn't make me feel like a failure, I felt accepted for who I am, and to this day all the friends I made there, and the few I met before Eagle, will always be my forever family.

Finally, here comes the day I have been waiting for my whole life, graduation day!! After ten months of long nights, tears, long days at work (and logging those paystubs for Mrs. Adams [ACE Program Coordinator]) I am finally going to be walking across that stage, that moment is something I will cherish for the rest of my life, it was my moment of realization that I was able to accomplish something nobody else thought I could do, greatest feeling ever. Since graduation I am now attending Arapahoe Community College, I will be graduating in the fall of 2017 with an associate's degree in Business Administration, but my education doesn't stop there; I will then be attending PIMA Medical Institute for Ophthalmic Medical Technician certification, which I will be graduating with an associate's degree there as well.

I just wanted to say thank you to all the staff at Eagle: Mama Rietsch, Mr. Hoaglin, Jay, Michalenko, Granat, Mr. Eberhardt, and last but not least, Mrs. Klinkerman. I love each and every one of you.
"The future belongs to those who believe in the beauty of their dreams"
~Gina Hines

ഝറ

Chapter Three – Those Itchy Labels

"You see us as you want to see us - in the simplest terms, in the most convenient definitions. But what we found out is that each one of us is a brain, and a basket case, a princess, and a criminal. Does that answer your question?
Sincerely yours, the Breakfast Club."

Not all students swear like sailors in an alternative education setting. For those of you whom have never set foot in an alt-ed building, some of the kids there do not fit the mold at all. There are the kids who are everything anyone hearing the title would expect: drug-users, smokers, multiple tattoos and piercings, dark clothing and multi-hued hair. Then there are the ones who needed an alternative to day school because of absences or illnesses, or in the case of one young lady, medical reasons. She was in a judo competition and had her back broken in a tournament. She opted to go to night school so she could pursue her pharmaceutical classes in the daytime.

Then there was a young man who was an international fencing champion who had missed so much school this was his best option for making up the missing credits.

Still more suffered from a disease that appears to be getting worse – social anxiety. I fully blame technology for turning us all into introverts, but that's another book. These students are so lacking in social skills and so overwhelmed by large crowds that they would just as soon NOT attend school than face an anxiety attack. The smaller class sizes in an alternative setting are much more appealing to them, and they find a home at Eagle and other alternative programs.

The ones who astonished me most are the ones who are the first to graduate from high school in their families. Yes, even in the year 2016, not everyone completes high school. I never knew this was an option as college was simply the given step after high school in my family. To this day I can't fathom why or how some would not complete high school,

∽の♋

but it does happen and even at Eagle. Though there are many, MANY nets in place to save even the most recalcitrant of students, there are the very few who just cannot "do" high school. Now, we teachers are supposed to save every single one of them, right? It can't be done when a student doesn't want it to be done. We even had a bottom "net" where students who didn't pass a class cooled their heels in Star Lab for nine weeks, and did their work in front of a computer, away from their friends. Most of the time this worked; sometimes it didn't and a student who had already been in there twice, or was rapidly approaching 21 years old, needed to be let go.

Think the Starfish Story. You educators all know it – you can't make a difference to all the starfish washed up on the shore, but you can make a difference to the ones you throw back in the water. When you have a student who decides to leave, you can beg, plead, and tell them they are making a huge mistake, but you can't save them. You can only show them you care enough to try to give advice. Ultimately, it is their choice (there's that word again), and if they were convinced a GED (General Equivalency Diploma) is what they wanted, you had to step aside. Truly, experience is the greatest teacher, and all you could say was, "I hope you don't look back on this with regret one day." And you lose sleep over students like that.

There is a great video by a teacher named Chase Mielke who voices his truth as a teacher who has also been "abused" and dissed, but who returns day after day to forgive and move forward. But even he has lost some, no doubt. It hurts. You forever wonder what you did wrong, what day you missed the opportunity to say something to let them know they mattered. You forget that they are human, just like they forget you are too, and that they have this thing called "free will". They can make choices that go against the very grain of your being, but it is their choice, their price to pay. Regardless of what the politicians and everyone else who has not spent a respectable amount of time in the classroom say, you can't save them all. You simply cannot make younger versions of human beings behave predictably.

The other part of the hallway/Foreign Language wing. The bulletin board was ours for job-postings and student awards. Good thing I took that bulletin-boarding class even though the counselor did all the work!

Teaching at a night school raised eyebrows because of the reputation, somewhat deserved, of alternative schools being "druggie schools." I have learned what students who had consumed something, other than food, over the dinner break looked like. Please note that these types of occurrences were not as commonplace as one would think. I think it was due to the many students who ended up in these halls understanding this was their next-to-last chance. They would mess up now and then, and habitual drug users were shown the door of a police car fairly quickly through no fault of the school's. They chose to do what they did in plain sight of the community around the school, and homeowners and businesses who wished to hang onto their property values would call the police.

Honestly, I wanted to hang my head and cry when Colorado approved marijuana for recreational use. Kids think "legal" applies to them, too, completely disregarding the age limits. Well, like alcohol, but much scarier in that pot's documented effects on developing brains is frightening. "But it's natural!" the kids would cry. Uh, no – the stuff you're insisting on using is nowhere near the "natural herb" it was years ago.

I had a student acting strangely one night, wanting to sit on the floor to read, and in general being overly polite and friendly. His eyes looked a little glazed to me, so I subtly moved in closer to see if I could smell anything. Another student who wanted to be a law enforcement officer one day slipped me a scrap of paper just as I passed the student on the floor. "That kid's in trouble" it read. I caught his eye and nodded imperceptibly, then went to find the principal and security guard. The student who had been on the floor turned up positive for prescription drugs and it turned out he had gotten into his dad's painkillers and some other drugs.

In a tragic turn of events, the student who handed me the note died inexplicably after staying up all night drinking Red Bulls and playing video games with another student. It was a student my husband had in middle school, so when he broke the news to me I burst into tears. The last words I ever spoke to this student were in the form of a question. "Hey, are we going to get you graduated?" I called after him as he walked down the hallway.

"I sure hope so," he smiled, and then left.

Going to student funerals is something I have done a few times in my career, three times now for students of the night school. Considering the amount of time I had spent there, three funerals over ten years is relatively few. Nothing will ever prepare you for that, and the possibility that you as a teacher will have to attend a funeral is never mentioned in teaching school. I had hoped, as all teachers do, to save this kid, but instead I watched with leaking eyes as the priest handed the little container of his ashes over to his stricken parents.

Another student who had been in my Senior Seminar class had gotten into quite a bit of trouble after graduating. She became pregnant, had a little boy, and what I last heard was getting clean. Then came the awful news she had died in her sleep; her heart apparently gave out. I drove myself to the funeral, crying the entire way to a friend because that year there had been multiple deaths in the surrounding schools, including my husband's, and I couldn't take anymore. I pulled off the side of the road and sobbed through the phone to another teacher friend. As it took me some time to pull myself back together, I was late to the

ॐ

funeral, and they had already moved her body to the cemetery. All I could do was sit in the empty church and cry.

I remain hopeful I will not have to attend another student funeral any time soon, but I am well-aware life does not always follow directions.

ഇരു

Chapter Four – Not-So-Recreational Use

"Students who went through DARE weren't any less likely to do drugs than the students who didn't. In fact, there's some well-regarded research that some groups of students were actually more likely to do drugs if they went through DARE." – from www.priceonomics.com, Oct. 2015

It was sadly comical to witness the kids who figure their drug use had helped them achieve enlightenment. They would pontificate about things they truly believe no one has pontificated about before, and therefore considered themselves far superior to most life-forms. All you could do is smile and nod, and then wait for them to resume their journey through education after they disappeared from class for a while.

Having policemen regularly visit your school wasn't a lot of fun, but it came with the territory. Each time it happened, you thought to yourself, *Well, there goes our reputation again.* Even though you knew most for the students were doing the right thing, it usually comes back down to that pesky free-will thing. And the state of Colorado legalizing marijuana didn't help one bit. A drug counselor once told the teachers at a staff development the kids really should be praised for "self-medicating" against their pain. Talk about mixed messages.

There was usually a last-minute private-to-the-staff announcement about the drug dogs coming sometime in the next hour. Thought I knew every precaution was made to keep the students from finding out, it seemed there was some type of radar instilled in those who had the most to fear. Suddenly they would sign out sick, as did a number of their friends.

There would come a knock at the classroom door, then we were told to step into the hall, leaving everything behind. The dog was brought in, usually one of those very intimidating German Shepherds with the solid black faces, and we would wait in the hall as the officers moved through the room. Some kids made quiet jokes, others looked petrified. Some grew indignant, and still others shrugged it off.

₧₨

I should have probably taken it more seriously a few times, but kids are kids, often lacking the frontal lobe connections to make predictions based off of their poor choices. They would show up to school stoned, thinking no one could tell or smell it on them, or for whatever reason, would keep all their paraphernalia with them. Getting caught could sometimes be the best thing that happened to them to save them from themselves. If not forever, at least for a little while.

There was a time during a drug-dog search that a student teasingly announced, "Klinkerman! The dog is alerting on YOUR stuff!" It was just one of those perfect jokes during a tense time, and I still have to suppress a smile when I think about it.

The new principal who arrived after my eight years there arranged for an anti-drug assembly, and it was probably the most uncomfortable choice of speakers we could have had. An affluent dad/son team, though some of my students swore they knew the duo were actually actors down at a little community playhouse. The father had talked about sending his drug-addicted son off to a facility, and the story had a happy ending, and now they went around to schools to give their testimony.

A parent at the end, whose daughter was still heavily using, was standing in the aisle, thinking of approaching the speakers, when she turned to me instead. "This is all well and good if you've got money, like he obviously does, but if you've got nothing, what do you do?" she snarled.

I asked if any of the low-cost programs were available in her area, but she shook her head. "They suck. They have constant staff turn-over, they don't take insurance, you never see the same counselor twice; it's like they don't care."

My heart sank. I could only offer lame suggestions of calling health insurance companies and searching for other programs as it was clear her daughter was in dire need.

Beyond a doubt there were quite a few other parents there that night feeling the same kind of hopeless. And when your entire state determines there is such a thing as legal drug use, how does one compete?

A Parent's Own Words:

When Albany, my daughter, came to live with my wife Marilyn and I at the age of 14, we were very comfortable with a cat and grandchildren. Taking on a teenager with a passion for pushing the boundaries of life and challenging herself by letting the world know it was NOT going to define her, was a bit disruptive.

Enrolling her in regular high school seemed like a good idea at the time. That is called "ignorance". I was needing, wanting, choosing to define my daughter by what I wanted her to be versus how she was presenting herself. Which is the same condition that created the circumstances of her finding her way to live with us! The subtle beauty within the chaos and struggle that was defining Albany would not be diminished, and in time the confining world of public school was taking its toll on her willingness to participate. [She could not] relate to the foreign world she attended in this normal educational curriculum which she had never fit in! All reflected in her grades and her frustrations in not being friends with the masses of students that were her peers.

One day Albany came to me and said she wanted to enroll in a special school within the current high school she was attending. I had never heard of such a thing and it was Albany that educated me. After her initial presentation, I was in no way supportive! I felt she was simply looking for an excuse to not show up and fit in! Wow! Talk about ignorance is bliss! The denial tea was strong, and I was drinking it daily. Even though I knew she was struggling every day of school, not going to some classes, not doing her homework, regardless of the parent portal, my constant involvement and seemingly supportive (controlling) role, I was adamant she continue and finish her regular schooling.

Being the persistent and strong young woman she is, Albany persisted and finally I gave an inch. I stated that she had to do the research and present to me and her school counselor that going to Eagle (the alternative school) would somehow be a better fit and beneficial to her education and that she would participate in attendance, homework, etc., rather than another diversion to avoid her life. I remember the morning we all met in the high school counselor's office and Albany presented her case. I don't remember her words; I do remember that when she was done talking I had nothing to offer to take away from her moving to Eagle for the rest of her schooling. Albany clearly and passionately presented her case. She had done her homework! Pun intended!

Within a matter of weeks, I was more involved in Eagle than I had ever interacted with the regular school. I met the teachers, the principal, AND the kids! They were all amazing! And somehow, surprisingly, no matter how bad this sounds, more authentic in all their weirdness (proper term - individuality) than any of the other kids I had met. Wow! My learning curve was steep, and yet I [became] a willing student to the students patient enough to accept me and allow me into their circle of conversations and even daily life. Smooth sailing, uh, no! But their approach and Eagle's approach was so much more personal and individual versus a cookie cutter response. When a personal situation or drama presented itself in Albany's life, I was more involved, engaged and felt a part of something personal, flexible and meaningful as opposed to a parent dealing with a daughter within a system of detail and structure. Albany was involved with a lot of the kids, not just one or two within the class. There was a sense of community within the kids. Yes, I experienced the dramas and issues typical of that age and social behavior, but even that felt different. The intensity at Eagle was more open and available; it could be seen, felt, and shared instead of glossed over and threatening if seen in public. These kids had come from tough situations and ended up at Eagle feeling they had nowhere else to go. Albany was there by choice.
~Thane Kraut

Chapter Five – More Greenery

"If you think in terms of a year, plant a seed; if in terms of ten years,
plant trees; if in terms of 100 years, teach the people."
~Confucius

Speaking of plants (pun intended), I had one in my classroom at
one point. I always admired the teachers who could keep live plants in
his or her room as I've never had much of a green thumb. I had a little
cutting of a Wandering Jew (or whatever the politically correct term is
for this plant now) that my daughter had given me as an elementary
school project for a Mother's Day present. I named him Froderick, and
brought him in to be the object to which the students must confess their
sins when caught cussing.

I had one student in particular who couldn't make it through a
single class without getting caught, and so his visits with Froderick were
quite frequent. While he was bombarding the plant with his apologies
for his transgressions, though, he would handle the spindly vines. He –
Froderick; not the student - started looking worse and worse. It was time
for an intervention, so I took the scraggly plant home.

Today Froderick is thriving in the corner of my kitchen and has
even been pruned back a few times. If you've never believed a plant
responds to how it is talked to, I have living proof of the truth of this
statement.

I have always admired those teachers that can keep a bevy of
plants alive in their classrooms. I just simply never got the hang of
caring for plants. There have been multiple studies reporting on the
benefits of having live plants in the classroom, and maybe one year I'll
try again, but in the meantime I'll have to plead "No contest".

In Their Own Words:
When I first started my journey at Eagle, I was 17. And a very lost
17-year-old at that. I was on probation, and was struggling with

＆⃝
problems in my personal life. I was flunking so behind in high school that I had no chance of graduating on time in a normal high school. That is when I decided on Eagle Academy. I wasn't expecting to take so much from the program, and, if I'm being honest, I figured it would just be a cop out for me to finish school. I couldn't have been any more wrong! Every class that was taught there gave you a whole new angle on its subject. Every teacher had a unique take on things. They were so passionate as well- after all, they chose to be there. They had a special way of passing that passion on to you, and I found myself caring about school in a way I never experienced before. I actually looked forward to school every day, and it allowed me to really learn things. I loved how everything was applicable to everyday life; how it was all so useful!

My first impression of the students, however, wasn't initially the best. I had assumed they were all like me- or worse. I figured they were careless, and even trouble makers. I soon learned that they were an evolved version of me. They had started out where I was. But they grew with the school, they matured and learned. Eagle helped prepare you for adulthood. They made you hold down a job. They gave you personal responsibility. We all needed that exposure. I think the majority of us would be so lost without it. Here I am, five years later. Doing what I love, being self-sufficient, and even planning my own wedding and soon my own family! While I can't tell you for sure where I'd be without the program, I know it wouldn't be this far. I wouldn't have been prepared. I would still be that lost teenager at heart. I am so thankful that Eagle came into my life when it did. It was a time when I really needed saving. And it definitely rescued me.
--Nicole Choromanski

ಐಂಟ

Chapter Six - Student Success Scores

"But there are advantages to being elected President. The day after I was elected, I had my high school grades classified Top Secret."
-Ronald Reagan

My last room at Eagle. I had two previous rooms over the years.

There was a system in place in our school called the Student Success Score, or SSS. It was basically what determined whether the student stayed on our classrooms, or spent the next quarter or nine weeks in the computer lab doing work online. There were three components: the student's academics for five points, his or her attendance for another five points, and finally the student's behavior for five points. Out of the 15, a student must maintain over nine points at the end of the quarter in order to continue. We used to factor in their work hours as we were considered a "program" by the state, so students had to be working during the day in order to be enrolled. We decided to count work hours separately around the time the economy took a nose-dive because students, and often their parents alongside them, struggled to find jobs. After also being audited by the state three times over work hours, this newer system kept records a little cleaner.

Without fail, at the start of each quarter, the more seasoned students started griping about the "newbies". Funny how quickly they forgot they were "new" once too, and another set of students was complaining about THEM. Students in alternative education get more passionately territorial of "their" school than I have ever seen in regular high school settings. I bring this up because it takes one quarter for the Student Success Score to act as the filter it was designed to be, and determine the fate of those whose bad habits followed them there. Students reemerged from STAR lab, and a new lot, who didn't understand Eagle is a REAL SCHOOL where attendance and doing your work really does count, move in. It was actually quite effective. Rarely did a student do more than two turns in there, but there were those that we simply could not reach, and those were the ones who often decided a GED was their best route.

Many of Eagle's students tried online school, ironically, and found it wasn't for them, that they needed "a body in front of them." I commended these kids for identifying what did not work for them and seeking an alternative format via Eagle. This was what made STAR lab so unappealing – the isolation. Who doesn't want to be around their friends? Granted some of our students with severe social anxiety did well there, but the smaller class sizes are what works in a program such as this. We kept classes to less than 18 in most cases as these kids had fallen through the cracks of an enormous class of 38 or 40 kids once; we couldn't let it happen again.

Teachers also pulled "Quintuple duty" in order to keep the classes small. No, that's not a typo. Where a regular high school teacher will teach one or two classes, maybe three, twice a week, alternative ed teachers will teach five to six classes one time EACH. I was in the six category as one of my 95-minute-long classes changed at semester. Plan periods? Not much; one period off on opposite days if you taught full time. We didn't meet on Fridays as this was our understood Plan Period. Truthfully, what kid in their right mind would show up on a Friday night? Plus this was when most of our food service employed kids made the most money.

My "planning period" fell on Tuesdays and Thursdays, Period 2. Even though it seemed like with smaller classes I'd be able to get all of my grading/lesson planning/website maintaining done in those off periods, rarely did this happen. There was almost always a student to console as they tended to wander in and out of class. It's not what you are thinking – very often the ability to roam is written in as part of their Individualized Education Program, or IEP. Students with severe ADD or ADHD or other behavioral disorders often have "free to move about or leave classroom" written in as an "accommodation". So forget having an off period if a student chose you to come in and talk to. This was a beautiful thing, really, but it was almost every off period I had where a student would need to come in and talk.

One student who came to visit one night told me he was struggling to keep up with the reading in another teacher's class. I asked him to tell me what the problem was after he went and retrieved the story. He said he had a "learning difficulty", and when he was reading would visually "flip my ps and bs".

I said, "I think you have dyslexia."

He said, and I'm still reeling from shock, "No one ever told me that before."

"Excuse me?" I sat back in my chair. "What grade are you in?"

"Eleventh."

Okay, so I was sitting with a student who clearly had a textbook case of dyslexia and was never told his in all his years in school. I sought the Special Education teacher in our building and demanded to know how this was possible. She explained that a school district cannot make evaluations like that because it requires costly medical testing that it can't ask the parents to do. When I picked my jaw up off the floor, I said, "So in the meantime it's okay to let the kid go through school believing he's stupid and incapable of learning?"

I stormed back to my room thinking this was the most useless, ridiculous notion ever if "experts" can get away with mystery diagnoses like "Learning disability" for everything from dyslexia to brain trauma.

I was still going to do right by this student, if for no other greater reason than the look of relief on his face that night. Sometimes being able to label something that is perplexing a human being can be a good thing. I tried him out on Dyslexie Font, a font developed to help people with dyslexia discern letters better. The look on that student's face said it all: *I'm not stupid; my brain and eyes just aren't working well together.* That alone was worth any amount of trouble I could get in for giving my professional opinion, what I thought I was trained for and paid to do.

In Their Own Words:
My name is Blaze Bennett. I came to arrive at Eagle Academy my junior year of High school. I felt that I could never really understand exactly what the teachers were trying to explain in class, and I was failing my classes because of it.

This school did so much for me, not only helping me graduate, but also taught me life experiences and how to handle situations no matter what it was. It also showed me that you can make friends with anyone no matter how different your lives may be.

My first impressions of the teachers were they seemed like they cared about the students and would go above and beyond to help you understand the material; it didn't seem like we were just another kid coming through the school. My first impression was just like anyone else's- it was going to a new school and not knowing anyone, but that didn't take long to make friends. [It was} not like most schools how kids would judge you on what you wore, or what you drove or any of that. They didn't care. It was about creating long lasting friendships that you could count on.

My impressions about the the teachers never really changed because as I got older it stayed the same. No matter how much you needed help, no matter what subject, it was the teachers would always help you out and the students would help you out also. My impressions about the students have changed some, but only because as some of the younger generation started to come to the school, it brought the mentality that "Oh, you didn't have a nice car" or "You dressed a certain

❧❧

way then we can't be friends." So the school started to have different groups of friends which it was never about before.

I have so much to owe all the staff and friends at Eagle Academy for where I am at today, I have my Associates Degree of Occupational Studies, and I have a great job working on cars for a living and doing what I love.

~Blaze Bennett

ഔ

Chapter Seven - Something Borrowed, Often Blue

"Everyday classroom teaching is not what children will remember, but how you made a difference in their lives."
-Nita Ambani

What you live and teach out of when you share a classroom.

Eagle Academy still does not have its own building, going on its seventeenth or eighteenth year, I believe. While everyone is screaming for charter schools and choice, and the district is finding money to build them, we kept on meeting in the day high school's Foreign Language Wing four nights a week. Let me tell you some of the fun we had sharing a building: We would get blamed for EVERYTHING. I mean, EVERYTHING. Something was missing from the day school? Our fault. Something was broken? Our fault. Graffiti on the bathroom walls? Those Eagle kids did it. Cigarette butts in the parking lot? Well, that one probably was our fault.

We were the convenient scapegoat. Nothing made us happier when something went amiss than finding out that it was a "day kid", not one of ours.

Some of the other problems we encountered were the heat and air conditioning were not in our control. Actually this is true for most school districts – the individual buildings are controlled centrally so there isn't any messing with the thermostat. The fun it presents when you don't have your own building is that at 3:00 in the summer months, the A/C gets turned off. There's no one there, right? Uh, wrong. There were nights so nauseatingly hot in our rooms that the principal released the kids early. (You can't open high school building windows for obvious reasons.) Other times, it was so cold you had to wear a sweater.

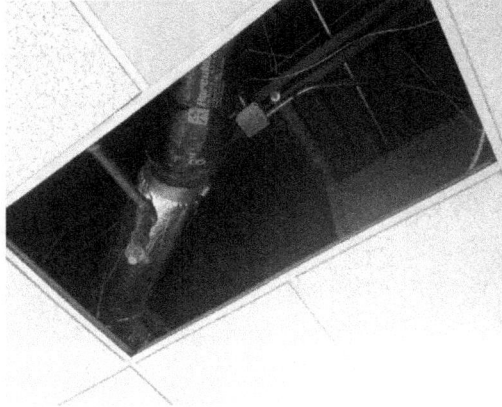

This was the missing ceiling tile and exposed HVAC system I taught under for at least three years.

Parking was always a problem as we night schoolers were pulling in when the day busses were supposed to be pulling out. When evening events overlapped, it was loads of fun to find parking. We were often locked out of the bathrooms because the day school kids did something to merit them as off-limits, and we would have to track down a key while our kids were standing cross-legged in the hallway.

On a more serious note, there was a problem with security. We had security guards, but the turnover rate was outrageous, and during one gap in security, an enemy of one of our students was waiting for him in the parking lot with a gun. The police came and took care of the matter, but I can assure you that trying to continue a lesson, when your room is lit up red and blue like a dance club because your window overlooked the parking lot, is a lost cause. At any given time, four to five of the seventeen entrances in the high school were wide open for evening events. Sure we practiced our intruder drills and such (a sorry state of affairs, if you ask me, that schools have to do this), but this wasn't exactly comforting.

We begged for some old locker space to use as a lounge for our kids as the lockers were no longer being used for the day school. We didn't get the proposed remodel because it was too expensive at a quoted $150K, but made due with the gated area for our kids to relax in and run their student store. After much cajoling on the new principal's part, we were finally granted that locker space from the day school. The students finally had at least one little corner in which to call their own.

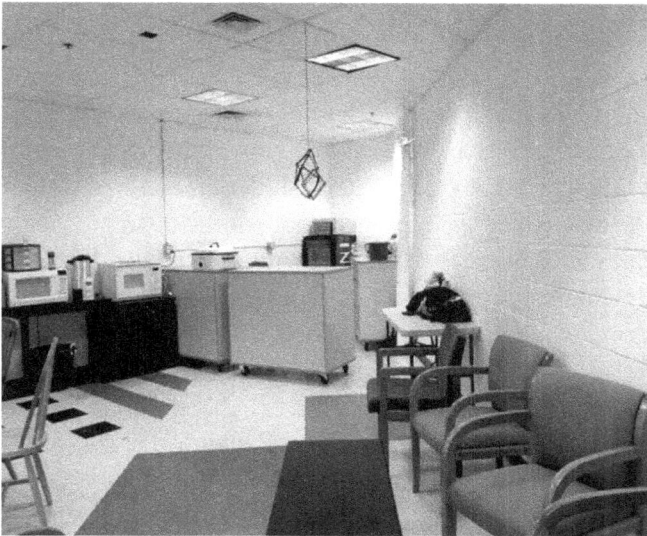

Lockers removed, we finally had a student lounge.

This was how we kept the day kids out, eventually earning that space the nickname "The Cage".

The ultimate insult was we didn't even get to use the day school's auditorium for graduation. We had to go down the road to another high school for our students to receive their diplomas. If there was a clearer message that we were the "stealth school" of the district, I don't know what it could have been. But we dealt with it. You just did. Even when the headline in the latest newspaper indicated the school district was looking to build five new charter schools.

Is the solution for Eagle to get its own building one day? That would certainly be a step in the right direction. And it has been requested, and denied, numerous times. The message *You don't count* comes through loud and clear, in my opinion, when having no real place to call home. These kids at least have a home in many teachers' hearts.

ଈଔ

Chapter Eight – Family Ties

"A family can be the bane of one's existence. A family can also be most of the meaning of one's existence. I don't know whether my family is bane or meaning, but they have surely gone away and left a large hole in my heart."
-Keri Hulme, The Bone People

The two senior-most staff members in the school were like an old married couple. They'd probably be the first ones to tell you that, too, even though both were married to other people. They were there the day Eagle Academy opened. As of the writing of this book, they are still there. We'll call the male teacher "J", though he'd readily admit to being the school's Curmudgeon, and the female teacher "Doc".

I learned very early on not to interfere with many of the systems in place, especially graduation plans because that was the couple's "baby". I nearly got my head bit off by Doc for trying to find larger graduation caps one commencement night. Actually, this was the second time Doc went off on me (more or less) in front of students. The first time was because I had crashed the one sad, Dell-infested computer lab (Ghetto Lab) for some Word processing when I had not realized she had signed up for it. In a state of shock, I left the school that evening in tears, and naturally ran into one of my more difficult students on the way out as I tried to hide my tear-stained face. He was sweet, saying, "Whatever it is, it will get better." Murphy's Law of Running into a Student When You Are Not at Your Level Best.

The next day I received a phone call as I was returning from giving a seminar. Doc apologized profusely, and later gave me a plant in front of a bunch of students. I have it in my home now as I learned I'm not a having-plants-in-the-classroom kind of teacher.

Doc is a cancer-survivor, I must add. In fact, twice now. Breast and thyroid. I guess I would be a little high-strung, too, facing such health issues, and I wish her all the best continuously.

The male part of the couple, J, was a sport-stat-spouting Rainman. Actually ANY stat. I said one night I was the third most senior staff member, and J corrected me in a hot minute, pointing out who had been there longer than I had been. I let him revel in his superiority for a moment before I leaned over and said, "I'm the third senior staff member in this room, so ha." (I can be a little competitive, too.) He could be so abrasive he made Comet Cleanser look like Soft Soap.

There were one or two "fun aunts" in the building, and though I *thought* I was, I was not one of them. English teachers with an abhorrence of bad spelling are not prone to praise until the student leaves.

The Fun Aunt who was the most impressive was "Ms. Manz" as the kids called her. She started up the school store, made meals for Doc's cancer treatment days, brought in food for the kids so they could eat dinner in her room and make up work they had chosen not to do for six weeks, ran marathons, and visited kids in jail. Yeah, I was a little jealous, but she was living a far different "paradigm" (a favorite word in the later years of my stint there) than I was.

As with any "family situation", work family or otherwise, you're not all going to love or even like each other at times. For the most part, though, we truly cared for one another. We would fight and make up (see above), eat together, problem-solve, and work through the latest educational trends together. A few of us hung out on weekends together, and a few of us avoided each other until the next workday. Perfectly normal.

When I was out interviewing for a new position during the day as my time at Eagle drew to an end, I was looked over time and time again. I was astounded. In a rare social mood, J put it simply one night: "You've got the Eagle Stain on you."

"What?" I stammered, incredulous.

It was the stigma, he explained. *Alt-ed teachers are less than.*

That got my ire up, I'll tell you. Let me be the first to put to rest, once and for all, the assumption that alternative education teachers are anything less than a "real" teacher. Or that we couldn't get jobs anywhere else. Every teacher everywhere, just like any regular human,

ಶೆ(ಿ)ಲ೯

has their own bizarre backstory, but we all come together for the sake of students, our most precious resources for the future.

    I had repressed knowing the stigma was out there, but I had been hoping other teachers on interview committees were above thinking that way. I was wrong, and it infuriates me that ANY teacher would look down on any other teacher. Especially those of us who were having wild successes with students other educators couldn't reach. (Irony.) Personally, I bow down to elementary school teachers as I KNOW for a fact I couldn't do that job.

ဢఁ

Chapter Nine – Passion for the Game

"A teacher must believe in the value and interest of his subject as a doctor believes in health."
-Gilbert Highet

I AM a tough teacher. I'm proud of it. I'm not mean; just insanely detail-oriented. I can spot a spelling error in a piece of writing at 100 yards. I'm a bad-a$$ Grammar Nazi, and the kids all knew it. No, I've never said to a kid, "Your writing sucks!" no matter how tempted I was.

Spelling errors will cost you in my classes, even today, but finding typos in other print pieces will earn you extra credit. I would rather be the teacher who drills proper spelling into kids than sharing my story-telling abilities with them. Think about it: there are far more web pages devoted to people who can't spell than there are sites devoted to people who can't do calculus. I rest my case.

The funny part is the kids, for the most part, appreciated my efforts and thanked me for making them better writers. They know I care, and that I am doing everything in my power to value them and make them better at communicating.

The opening to my class was a modified Route To Intervention (RTI) practice where I arranged my desks in a circle and kids get the first few minutes to Rant or Rave or Reply to a question I asked. I passed a little Talking Stick I received from a Seven Habits of Highly Effective People class I took. What I learned about alternative education kids is they NEED something to manipulate. Even just holding the object was a connection to the little community to which they belonged as the kids passed it from hand to hand. Everyone's touch left an invisible mark to be absorbed by the next student.

Eugene the Zombie Talking Stick

With my apologies to Franklin Covey, when I left the course, which was really very informative, we are all given these resin talking sticks. In my opening of class/Restorative Practice circle, I let the kids pass "him" around. I say him because, like Froderick, I had to come up with a unique name, so I chose Eugene. I wrote it on the bottom of the base in green Sharpie.

Each night, the kids would pass Eugene around, and he would get tapped on desks, or dropped, but he held his own. Until that one fateful day he made contact with the edge of a desk and broke in two. We all sat there in silent disbelief, looking at the pieces on the floor.

"That did NOT just happen," someone finally said, and stunned laughter followed.

I had Superglue at home, so Eugene's pieces were tucked in my book-bag, and we found a replacement "Talking Stick" drumstick to pass around for the rest of the night.

Sadly, Eugene now had a weak spot, and when he fell a second time a month later, the two pieces lay sadly looking up at the circle. (Uh, Superglue? Your product NEVER holds what I need it to hold.) I packed him up once again, but this time I brought the Superglue back to school in case the tragedy occurred a third time.

Well, it did. I decided that Eugene had been brought back from the dead so many times that he was officially a zombie. A little red nail polish dripping from his repaired break, and his multiple pairs of eyes and numerous mouths, and presto – you have the picture you see here. Little did my kids know that my sense of humor could be so gruesome. They loved it. Eugene, I am proud to say, made it through the rest of the school year without another mishap, and now stands guard over my day school desk.

Around that circle, I heard some fascinating and tragic details of lives that I cannot fathom. There have been tears and laughter, we've found work for those looking, and even almost had a dog adopted. The student's mother ended up giving the dog away while the student was at work and before the boy who wanted it could take it in. Some days I listened intently, other days I shook my head that all that seemed foremost in students' minds was getting enough money to go to the next Pretty Lights show. (It really is a thing.) I had a few students who rarely said anything, but being able to grasp Eugene, even for just a moment as they passed it, lent itself to some connectedness, even if the student had not verbally contributed. And students expressed how grateful they were that I did this.

"No teacher has ever listened to me like this," they said. I was quick to try to back up regular day school teachers in over-crowded classrooms by reminding the kids that they didn't have this luxury, that what they do is more like "crowd-control" when there is a body in every single desk (and then some) in the room.

At the last graduation ceremony I was part of as staff, a student took his two minutes at the microphone and spoke of the Rants, Raves and Replies. In a heartfelt speech where he addressed a few other teachers and how much they cared, he said, "…And then there's Ms. Klinkerman who cares so much about you that right when you walk in to her classroom she has what's called Rants and Raves, where if you had her class you know that basically you talk about your day. And talking about your day with her, and how much she cares about you, just makes you feel better, even if you had a crappy day. If you're having a great day, it just makes it better."

Large or small, the Circle took in all.

Chapter Ten – Education Idiosyncrasies

"Nothing could be as hard as middle school."
~ Zooey Deschanel

Speaking of middle, I taught in middle school for ten years because of a mistake. Hear me out, new teachers; I never aspired to be a middle school teacher. You see, it was the first job I was offered and I accepted. I had not even applied to high school though I had known all my student teaching days that I strictly wanted high school. Well, once you choose your grade level, you get pigeonholed there, and from then on you are assumed to be a middle school teacher, elementary teacher, or high school teacher. I could not get a high school position no matter how hard I tried. It was maddening. I recall many high school interviews where I was asked specifically if I coached any sport. "Uh, no," I would say tentatively, knowing with that one response my chances of being hired went right out the window. I had no idea what a big deal high school sports were until moments like those.

If you want to teach high school, you'd better be able to coach something. Getting double and triple duty out of one teacher is completely the norm. Sure they pay you for your extra duty, but it's rarely more than $1500. The only reason I know this is I helped coach middle school football for a season. Yes, me. Really, all I did was stand there, but they needed an extra body on the field because so many kids had signed up. And if you think there are a lot of middle school girl tears, you've never seen middle school boys involved in a sport.

So I settled into being a middle school teacher, and was considered one for a decade.

At another interview for a high school within the last ten years, and a .3 position at that, which is maybe one class, the principal himself told me that having a college degree doesn't even matter anymore. I about gagged, sitting there with my Master's Degree. "All you need are 24 units in your area and you are considered 'Highly qualified.'" Believe me that revelation had me in a whirlwind of confusion, wondering why I had wasted so much time getting degrees, and thinking to myself, "Great – my daughter may have a teacher that never graduated from college." Not that there aren't famous people who never graduated from college, but THEY were mostly taught by people who did.

This segues nicely into a little bit about what's going on in education these days with programs like "Teach For America". I don't believe in it. The end.

Seriously, what is the use of offering bonuses for corporate-to-classroom teachers who on average only last three years? Here is a program that needs to be scrapped if I ever saw one. As I have already mentioned, nothing, but NOTHING will prepare you for your first year of teaching, and if you even make it past your third year, then and only then are you getting your classroom management skills under control. According to EdWeek.org from a study in 2014, "After five years, 27.8% (of Teach For America teachers) were still in teaching. This retention rate is markedly lower than the 50% estimated for new teachers across all types of schools (Smith & Ingersoll, 2003)." I'm no math major, but can you see where this is a problem?

Chapter Eleven – Sharing is Caring, So Play Nice

"Oh, you can't help that," said the cat. "We're all mad here."
~Alice in Wonderland

Did I mention Eagle not having its own building? What I may have failed to address was the necessity of making friends with your roommate. Technically, it's the day teacher's room. You were just borrowing it at night. We kept our supplies in cabinets, and when you were getting ready to start your evening, you just unlocked them, and then at the end of the night, locked them back up again. You were like ghosts, no-trace campers, vampires. Now you see us; now you don't. Again, it often felt convenient to only acknowledge Eagle's existence when something went wrong, or there was a requirement to be met.

There were moments, though, when "the twain shall meet." I would see my day school roommate at the end of her day, the beginning of mine. We became friends, but it took a few years of pleasantries to establish this relationship. A few of my colleagues, never seemed to have established a good relationship with their roommates. I spent a semester as a "traveling teacher", meaning all of my gear was on a rolling cart and I would go room to room in a - you guessed it - middle school, so I know what it means to quickly establish rapport with the teacher in whose room you are "guesting".

When you are technically a traveling teacher, much like a substitute you hang out in the staff "lounge" until quite certain "your" room has been vacated.

My roommate became my friend, especially due to my other female friend leaving for greener pastures a few years back. She shared quite a bit about her dating life, which at first made me uncomfortable, but then became a normal routine.

There were a few times I had to motion to the doorway that students could not yet come in as she was relaying a recent development. Teachers always think that students don't realize they have a private life, and don't recognize an animated personal conversation when they see one. I thought so, too, until a former day-turned-night-school student who had her as a teacher said, "Sounds like Ms. XYZ is having boy troubles again." Sometimes teachers let being human show.

I entered "my" room after one Christmas Break to find a giant, eye-boggling mural had been painted on the back wall by the Junior Honors Society. (See photo from earlier.) The geometrics and the giant falcon were enough to make your head spin, but again, it was clearly not my place to say anything about it. This was not my room, not my wall.

I've dealt with broken desks, some of which had probably been in that room for a decade, and I taught under a missing ceiling panel for at least three years. (It is probably still missing.) I could look up and see all the heating vents and electrical. Goodness knows what that 25-year-old dust blowing down on me night after night was doing to my health, but no one seemed to be in a hurry to fix it. We couldn't control our heat and A/C anyway, as is practice with most school districts. There were afternoons when we would enter the building to find it already stifling from the heat of 30+ bodies in the rooms half an hour ago, and the A/C would be shut off because it was after 3:00pm. Remember, school building windows do not open for obvious reasons, so there was no escaping the sweltering heat. In desperation I moved my class (more than once) out into the hallway to sit on the somewhat cooler linoleum. Mercifully, the former principal would let us all leave on nights like that because no one could concentrate with sweat rolling down their cheeks anyway.

ဆာ

Chapter 12 - Stories from The Circle

"I have learned that delivering the best possible palliative care to children is vital, providing children and their families with a place of support, care and enhancement at a time of great need is simply life-changing."
~Kate Middleton

Oddly, it seems more men than women teach in alternative education settings, the polar opposite of most day schools. This is a boon to the students as boys outnumber girls in this setting at least three to one. And heaven knows they often need a strong male role model. The stories I heard about the father figures in these kids' lives would cause me, on more than one occasion, to remind myself to keep my mouth closed.

There was the story from one of my students whose brother was living in the family's basement with the pregnant live-in girlfriend. The brother couldn't handle the fact that he was going to be a father and could therefore no longer smoke pot, so the father gave him some. Thank you, Colorado.

Another student told me his parents took trips with his siblings, often leaving him at home alone. Still other fathers would appear at Parent/Teacher conferences looking very much like the commercial methamphetamine addict; rotted teeth, gaunt, wearing a strung-out expression. (You've got to love the addicts who truly believe no one can tell.) This is definitely one of those moments when you would prefer the school suddenly become a boarding school. Multiple times I said I wished we had fold-down cots on the walls so kids could just live there because their home lives sounded so terrible. Granted this was teenagers with an aptitude for dramatics, but in many instances it wasn't. The apple does not fall far ENOUGH away from the tree in many cases, and some of our little apples you wanted to kick just so they would roll farther.

ॐ

A rather risky writing prompt I used in the past asked if people should have to obtain licenses to have children, and every single one of my charges would emphatically agree that being determined to be qualified to be a parent in the first place was a good idea. Their stories were enough to convince me this really might be a good idea no matter how hard to implement.

There are two sides to every story, of course – the truth and a teen's side. However, the stories they regaled me with were so outrageous they had to be true. Except when it came to cop stories. Those I am certain didn't go down anywhere close to what the kids were telling each other and me. Cops were simply "out to get them", and had ego problems, power-trips, you name it, and they were taking out on the kids. I know there is a distinct possibility the cops were really acting like that as I have seen firsthand how these kids talk to their own parents. I would not be surprised that whatever they were dishing out to a cop was earning them all kinds of "disrespect" back.

I once watched a young man berate his father for not reminding him to bring his missing make-up work back to school. It's funny how kids will take no responsibility for their actions, but yet want to be trusted with operating a 3500-pound chunk of hot metal filled with flammable liquids. "You are actually allowed to drive a vehicle?" I blurted when he told me he had forgotten his work for the millionth time. I know; shame on me. No sarcasm in the classroom. Bad teacher. But believe me you'd resort to this kind of snark, too, of you listened to some of those same stories on what felt like eternal repeat. As many teachers learn, YOU grow older, but the kids in your classrooms do not. They will forever be in that grade level, with the same issues and the same stories and the same personas, if you stay there. If you leave and then return to the same grade, it is not going to be much changed. That's the funny thing about school - education trends may change, but the kids do not.

ಶಂಗ

Chapter 13 - The Bomb Scare

"All over the world, young males and females, schooled in the art of
patriarchal thinking,
are building an identity on a foundation that sees the will to do
violence as the essential way to assert being."
~ Bell Hooks

I drove into the parking lot one cold afternoon to see kids milling about. A quick glance at the clock confirmed I was not late, so something was up. I spotted my colleagues and asked what was going on, and they reported they had been evacuated from the building for some reason. The day kids were released ten minutes early, but most of the buses were not yet there. Our students were arriving, and seeing that they weren't going to be let into the building, some opted to just leave.

Police cars were amassing on the campus, and they security guards yelled for the kids to get away from the building. As most of the day school teachers had also left, we night school teachers herded the kids across the parking lot to the safe zone to load the buses from that side. Pretty soon whispers of "bomb" started circulating. As it turns out, that afternoon security found scribbles on the bathroom mirror of some type of threat against the school. For the third time. (Be friends with the security guards – you'll find out a lot more that way.) This time was enough to finally call in the sheriffs, and an hour and a half later it was determined a thorough search with bomb-sniffing dogs needed to be conducted.

Time passed. Earlier I moved my car so two freezing girls (no jackets, of course) could sit inside and get warm. Other students were begging to go to the bathroom, to which most of us teachers said, "We can't stop you – just go!" Most returned, and most students stayed as this was supposed to be their third quarter finals night. Nearly two hours later the principal called the students to gather and explained the sheriffs weren't going to clear our wing any time soon so finals would be conducted after Spring break. Now most of us teachers would have been happy posting grades as-is, due to uncontrollable circumstances, but apparently he did not see it that way. And, naturally after a week off, the kids arrived back to take their finals and did dismally.

As it turned out, the culprit of the threats was a ninth grader looking to get out of a quiz. Or so the security guards told me. Reward money was posted, and the kid, thinking he and his friend could split the loot, suggested his friend turn him in. Ah, the sweet bliss of lacking a frontal lobe to aide in predicting when what you are about to do will have lifetime repercussions.

Being locked out of stuff wasn't really a new thing when you shared a building. Repeatedly the bathrooms were locked on us due to some day school mischief. That was always fun – wondering where and when you were going to be able to pee. As if teachers haven't already learned how to hold it for unreasonably long stretches of time. We had keys, and often we simply had to track them down and unlock the restrooms, but at times it was a plumbing problem. More than once the janitors (also to be made your friends as quickly as possible) told me the day kids were thinking it hilarious fun to stuff apples and oranges down the aging building's plumbing.

Are office restrooms this luxurious?

ഹാരു

Weather plays a part in determining a night school's operations on occasion. Bitter cold and icy roads are challenging, and teenagers can't drive well in good weather. Early release nights used to be the best when our old principal still ruled the roost. The minute he would get the call from district, that is IF he got the call as often we were forgotten, class would be over. The new principal simply made the announcement, rearranged class times, and expected us to continue with a shortened schedule with kids about out of their minds with wanting to leave.

In Their Own Words:
    I started at Eagle in October of 2005. I decided to attend Eagle because I got pregnant at 16. Eagle allowed me to stay home during the day with my son and finish high school at night. I graduated in January of 2007, six months ahead of when I would have graduated from high school if I had stayed in a traditional school. All of the teachers there were supportive and understanding. I remember having a babysitter cancel on me a few times and the teachers welcomed me and my son to class those days. Everyone was supportive, respectful, understanding, easy to talk to. I definitely feel like Eagle and all the amazing teachers there have helped to better my life.
~Kim Allen

ଛଠଇ

Chapter 14 - A Birthday To Remember

"I work on holidays. I work on birthdays. I work on New Year's. I work. I keep my ears to the streets."
~ Juicy J

It was my birthday week, but after about 25, and especially in education, that doesn't really matter much. No one sings to you or brings in cupcakes (if those are even allowed in the classroom anymore), and you absolutely don't take the day off. As I may have mentioned before, a teacher would rather be bleeding out both eyes and both ears before calling in sick. A teacher can't just think their work will be there when they get back as you are dealing with a bunch of living, breathing beings that need constant care and attention. Having to explain the little nuances of the classroom in substitute plans is a pain in the behind, so more often than not, teachers of any classroom type will go to work on their deathbed. For an alternative classroom, teachers will pull themselves out of the grave if they have to just to not have a substitute in the room who the kids may or may not eat alive. So taking the night off for your own birthday? No way, no how. The wizard needs to be there.

The week started out with a giant drug bust, a student's second offense and therefore subsequent expulsion. The principal pulled us into his office, saying, "I want you to see what your kids have been doing."

I was immediately offended, thinking, "MY kids?"

What he meant was the students of Eagle Academy. We walked into his office to see his little round conference table covered with drug paraphernalia. A giant jar of marijuana, vape pen attachments, a Baggie of weed, scales, and a notepad and pens. Thank you, again, Colorado, for making weed legal.

Wednesday, my birthday. My long night, meaning no plan period. I had exactly a half hour for dinner, and my husband wanted to bring me one of my favorite meals. He came in with pho, and we set up two desks to sit and shovel food in our faces while frantically catching up on the day. He even had a little cake for me.

As time grew short, he went to clean up before my last period of the day came in, and in came a girl looking shell-shocked. I asked her what was wrong, clearly seeing her red-rimmed eyes and pale face. She said, "I just made the biggest mistake of my life."

I have had students in my room before telling me similar stories, but they were more along the lines of falling from their sobriety. I was not at all expecting what she was about to tell me. I had already instinctively gathered her into my arms by then, and whispered, "Whatever it is you can talk to me about it."

She replied, "I had an abortion."

The words to comfort her dissolved. This was a situation I was not prepared for, and what do you say anyway? She had asked if she could sit in the hallway, and I let her go.

My husband, who had seen me holding the girl and wisely waited in the hall, then came back and asked me, "What was that all about?"

"She had an abortion," I answered.

He closed his eyes and said, "My God. What is she doing here?"

"We are her 'normal'," I said simply because I knew it to be true.

School is, a lot of times, the 'normal' for a child. It bears repeating. The stories I have already discussed, to the aforementioned moment, make school with its boring rows of desks and drab halls, tired lessons, clanging bells and rigid rules seem like a haven for students who have less-than-ideal home lives.

The following afternoon, the weather in Denver was growing ominous. Our policies were such that if the day schools called off afternoon activities due to weather, we would also close. It was looking like a mere matter of time before we were sent home.

The principal was away for some personal time, leaving our Building Resource Teacher in charge. The snow was dumping down outside the windows, and the cars in the parking lot were beginning to disappear under a layer of white. Students always get squirrely when the weather changes, but they were inconsolable as they walked in after their dinner break.

"When are we going home?"

"It's getting really bad out there!"

"This is dangerous!"

"Why haven't we been let go yet?"

I assured them I was not the one in charge, and we were waiting to hear from the district level people when we could leave.

Finally, the voice of our BRT (Building Resource Teacher) came over the loudspeaker and announced we would be released in a half hour. Goodbye, student focus and lesson plans. I wisely chose to let them send quick texts to their rides and friends, then opted to read out loud to them in hopes of keeping their excitement levels under control.

The clock struck the designated minute, and the kids tore from the room. I wanted to get on the road myself as I had one snow-related accident that had scarred me forever. However, in walked a student begging for a ride home.

I am certain my face registered my dismay, but so did hers. I asked, incredulous, "Your dad won't come get you again?" This poor kid was constantly getting rides from teachers because her own father, for whatever his reason, wouldn't. I had already driven her home twice this school year, out of my way by at least 20 minutes one direction. And now in the snow?? I really did not want to be liable for this student, but her regular teacher ride couldn't, which left me no choice. Her second staff ride option WAS the acting principal, and that night she had to stay to ensure all the kids had vacated the school.

I was not happy. Not in the slightest. I'm a native Californian and a nervous wreck on snowy roads after one accident my first year in Colorado. But duty called, so I packed up the student, said a prayer under my breath, and hit the road.

An hour later, I finally found myself back at home, shaking like a leaf, and about as tense in the shoulders as one could get. The student prattled nearly the entire ride to her home, and I fed her prattling by asking questions so I wouldn't have to drive in awkward, slushy silence. Part of me had wanted to walk her to her door so I could meet her father myself, but the other part of me knew she was embarrassed enough about her situation. I kept my opinions locked behind a bitten tongue.

So much for my birthday week when visions of pedicures and massages usually dance through my head...

සටඹ

Chapter 15 – The Moments You Live For

"Education is the key to success in life, and teachers make a lasting impact in the lives of their students."
~ Solomon Ortiz

There was another student I somehow connected with though our worlds were miles apart. It actually isn't that great of a mystery- we both loved House music- EDM, or Electronic Dance Music.

Before the Christmas break, I had heard he and his family were in a bad way. His and another student's, I should correct. There was a really good chance that Christmas dinner was going to be dismal at best. The teachers discussed getting these students in a program to deliver meal boxes or something, but I decided to approach my local grocery store for gift cards at my mom's suggestion. I knew the manager since I had been shopping there for years, and I had written a glowing letter about their customer service due to an incident years earlier. (The short version of the story was an employee went to get my car for me in a rainstorm so my then-infant daughter and I wouldn't drown in the struggle to get groceries in the car. I won't shop elsewhere. Thank you, King Soopers grocery.)

The manager gave me two gift cards, each for $20.00, and I anonymously sent them to both students in time for the holidays.

The second semester passed, and it was graduation day for both students. The student I had connected so strongly with was taking pictures with his family after graduation, and was standing proud in his cap and gown, with an unusual cord of flowers and twisted palm fronds around his neck. I approached and congratulated him and his family, but the curiously of what had happened to the gift card was nagging at me. I had to know.

"By the way, did you get an anonymous gift card in the mail around Christmas time?"

His face went from not registering, to lighting up, to overwhelmed in an instant. "That was you?? Oh, my God!" He clapped his hands to the sides of his head and announced this fact to this family.

I was instantly swarmed, tackled with hugs, backslaps, and handshakes, overwhelmed expressions of gratitude like I had never seen. Christmas Dinner would have been nothing without that unexpected gift. The student lifted the flower lei from his neck and draped it around mine. My eyes welled up and my throat constricted as my hands went up in protest.

"No," he said, "This is for a person of honor in my culture."

It's dried and faded now, but I will keep it forever.

This will always have a special place.

ॐ

Chapter 16 - Parent/Teacher Conferences

"Every child should have a caring adult in their lives. And that's not always a biological parent or family member. It may be a friend or neighbor. Often times it is a teacher."
~ Joe Manchin

Before Parent/Teacher conferences, we would have a potluck dinner. There was not time to go out and grab something, obviously, so all afternoon of shortened classes, we would be smelling things simmering in crockpots. If you have never seen teachers throw a potluck, we can do it better than anyone. Our then-principal was a master barbeque-er and meat-smoker, so tender shredded pork and beef ribs were always the mainstay, and the rest of us would fill in with salads and sides, desserts and beverages. Non-alcoholic, though it may have helped.

We would have a cake for any staff members whose birthdays were that month, and we would share stories and concerns about students as we ate. Forty-five minutes for dinner was considered a luxury on these nights, though without fail there would be parents who showed up a half-hour early to see if they could get in before everyone else. No matter how impatient they looked, we would continue eating behind a closed door because we had so little staff time together, and this was our only chance. Our rare time to feed our own souls by making stronger connections to each other before putting the battle armor back on and heading to the frontlines.

Really, parent conferences are something to behold as they explain a lot about students. But in this alternative setting, even more would be revealed. An ugly divorce situation. A parent who clearly had a drug problem. An adoptive situation. A guardian in charge of a younger sibling because the parents were no longer in the picture.

Many times, though, the parent, guardian, or parents, would come in and just cry. They had never seen grades that good before, and they were overwhelmed with happiness and relief that their child was finding success. These were the truly rewarding meetings. Often students themselves would not be there as they had already been to school once that afternoon so they were unlikely to return. When they did, though, it was time to ask them my one patented question: "Are YOU happy with what is going on with your grades?" A smile was all the answer I'd need.

Ownership is a huge thing for students in almost every grade level, although shirking this responsibility is very convenient. But these students, I personally felt, needed to quit blaming others for their shortcomings, no matter how crappy their home lives were, and come to school to give it his or her best. To be truthful, that rarely happened at first for many students. "D for Diploma", some would say, and I would beg them to aim higher than that. Some took my words to heart, and for that I was grateful.

As to the level of "rigorousness" in an alternative program, yes, we made it fairly easy for kids who had jobs during the day to not have to struggle too much at night. Homework was not assigned. Just be there and get your work done. Pretty simple. The fact of the matter is many of these students did not plan on going to college, and the ones who did definitely stood out. You knew it by his or her work ethic. I have had students declare they were going to be a ski lift operator for the rest of their lives, and I would shake my head, but if they were content doing that, so be it. College isn't for everyone, contrary to every teaching bone in my body.

But then the miracle would happen: a year or two years later, I'd get a social media note from a former student. "Hey, guess what, Boss K? I'm going back to school!"

Happy teacher.

Sometimes we got out and saw the sun. Literally and figuratively.

&)(3

Chapter 17 – Interview: A Parent's Perspective

"At the end of the day, the most overwhelming key to a child's success is the positive involvement of parents."
~ Jane D. Hull

Facebook is a wonderful thing, on occasion. It helps me keep up to date with my former students in a way I would have never guessed possible. Kids from my early years as a teacher in California, to my most recent graduates from Eagle Academy. I can see which of them are landing new jobs, getting married or celebrating birthdays, having their own families, and even the nights some are struggling with their depression.

Not too long ago, I was in need of a new hairdresser as my misguided notions of a get-by haircut landed me in dire straits. I recalled at least two of my former graduates were now running their own businesses as stylists, so I chose one (don't worry – I will have my husband visit the other one as her specialties are men's cuts) to fix the bargain haircut I received, and also to give my daughter a badly needed trim.

I walked in to her new salon to find her mom there getting her hair colored. Basically, I could not believe my luck as getting parent contributions for this book have been a little difficult. Grabbing opportunity by the horns, I asked if I could interview her and she agreed, foil in her hair and all.

Shelley West, Morgan's mom:
How did it come to pass that alternative education was a better fit for your daughter?
The struggles she was having at [her old high school]. She had a friend already there at Eagle, and it basically started at [former high school] conferences. Things weren't working and she was falling behind. There was a distinct lack of connect, a feeling of overwhelm, and feeling like she was going to give up. It wasn't working mainstream.

ಬಂ

How long was she at [former high school]?

Two years. She played rugby there, so that was about the only thing she missed.

What were your first impressions when you went through the interview process to get in to Eagle?

I was impressed with the obvious relationships between students and staff; you could tell it was more one on one. She felt she had more support available, and she felt more comfortable. I saw the pressure lift off of her. It seemed like a big difference, more personal, and that is what she needed. A smaller, more personal environment.

Knowing where we live and work, having a kid at an alternative school is not the norm. What were the reactions you received?

Well, being in Highlands Ranch, [Colorado] no one wants to step out of the box. I got some questions as to whether she was getting a quality education (at Eagle Academy), but I saw the difference in her. As a parent, you do what is best for your kid. The depression lifted, and she opened up more. School wasn't such a burden. She didn't fight going to school and it was more of a fit for her personality.

As I didn't know much about it when we started, I wondered a lot if it was the right decision. It was a gradual change in her where she seemed happier. This was just a load off of me. No more worries about her quitting school altogether, which every parent worries about. You never know what is going on in their minds.

How about her life now?

The relationships she made at Eagle built her confidence, and now she's a mom and a business owner at 24 years old. The positive outcomes and success there made a big difference. It is just so hard for some of these kids these days (to fit in), and with her personality it made all the difference. As a parent, I can only say you have to get past that stigma, the alternative label and put your child where they will see success.

∞⊃⊂∞

Morgan in her own words:

One of my best friends moved to Eagle a couple of semesters before me and with what I was going through at my old high school (Never wanting to go, having problems with the class size, always falling behind, etc.) it seemed like the best choice for me to go to Eagle.

My first impressions of Eagle was nothing I'd ever expect. Everyone was so nice and welcoming and best of all, nothing like my old high school. Another great thing is that everyone was treated like family.

Every time I reflect on my memories of Eagle, each one is filled with pure joy. As I'm getting older there's nothing I wouldn't do to be able to go back and re-live it all over again. I sincerely feel if I had not gone to Eagle, there's a very good chance that I wouldn't have graduated or even gotten my GED. I had no thoughts of what would happen after high school, and Eagle most definitely gave me hope for that chance of a real high school diploma.

Now that I've graduated (A mere six years ago) I became a mother to the most precious baby girl, completed beauty school, and most recently opened my own studio of my own! I'm so thrilled that Eagle gave me the chance to become something. I honestly don't know what I (as well as many others) would've done without the help of everyone at Eagle.

And thank you to each of the staff from the bottom of my heart for believing and pushing all of us "delinquent" kids.

~Morgan West

PS- For the record, I was the one who nicknamed you, Boss K.*

(*You know you've arrived when your kids nickname you.)

℘ℭℛ

Chapter 18 - The Year (almost) Without an Eagle Academy

"I want to go working with good people on something that's good, because otherwise it's a big waste of time. I don't have that much time."
~ Stockard Channing

After my first year at Eagle, I was without a job. The position I had taken was only for one year, and by that time I had fallen deeply in love. My last night, right after graduation I broke into tears in the bar where we were having an end of the year beverage. I think I cried all the way home.

I spent the next year substitute-teaching at Eagle, and at the beginning of August, I received a call from the principal, asking if I would be interested in teaching a class for seniors to help them get through that critical first year of college.

"I can't think of anyone better than you to create this class," Doug Seligman said over the phone, and so I was back as a .2 teacher at Eagle. I was entrusted to create the curriculum for a class titled Senior Seminar, so I borrowed heavily from new classes in community colleges designed to do the same thing.

A quick glance at US News and World Report's Education website reveals the retention of first year college students in the state of Colorado averages less than 70%. These students are even less likely to return because they cannot find their way around the system. "Despite the growing need for increased education and advanced degrees to secure jobs, only 59 percent of students who begin college as freshman at a four-year college receive their diploma within six years. Students who come from low-income backgrounds are even less likely to graduate—if they even begin at all", according to the online edition of the Washington Post, October 23, 2014.

Senior Seminar was born, and it was by far the most fun class to teach. The very curriculum took me back to my college days, perhaps my most favorite in my educational career. (I haven't sought out my doctorate yet, but maybe one day…) If nothing more, helping to prepare fledgling adults to head off into the world is a teacher's greatest mission.

A colleague surprised me twice with an activity she did at the end of the quarter with her charges, and that was to get them to write a Thanks to their teachers at the end of the quarter. I have kept the sometimes backwards compliments in the back clear pocket of my attendance binder as testament to my teaching abilities. (Very useful to read on those less-than-perfect days.) The compliments vary: *"Mrs. Klinkerman frustrates me but in the best way possible. She has very high expectations and she wants her students to give it 110%. … Mrs. Klink is a lioness; she's a winner, and honestly she kicks ass"* (My personal fave.) Or this one, apparently making a student *"redheaded with frustration because I don't like writing"*, but he respected what I was doing. Then, the ultimate: *"You have helped me find a side of school I never thought I would find. Success."*

I never really understood what my dad would say when I was growing up – "You may not like me but you will respect me" – until I became a teacher. No, I may never earn a warm-fuzzy award for my teaching, but I don't mind being respected by my students for pushing them. Teachers do not get into the profession to become friends with their kids. We are more like athletics coaches than instructors these days anyway. As it was said, gone are the days of being "The Sage on the Stage"; we now must be "The Guide on the Side". Or as my colleagues and I back in Santucky (Santee, California) used to say, "We're more like 'The Diddle in the Middle'."

In my time at Eagle Academy, I created the curriculum for two more reading classes, including English Strategies II and English Survey. I was allowed to choose books I determined to be of high interest for these, the most reluctant of readers. I was right in my perceptions, and had students who "hate" reading thank me for awakening their desire to read again. Here are just some of the comments I have received:

Mrs. Klinkerman, I am liking the second book we are reading. I have never been so interested in treading. You always pick out the good

ℬℭ

books so we don't get bored during class. Thanks for being that fun English teacher. ~Pepper

Mrs. Klinkerman, I wanted to thank you for all the things that you helped me with this year. English has never been one of my favorite classes. You have made it so I don't mind writing as much as I did before. I also wanted to thank you for the patience that you had with me. You really do a lot for the students here at Eagle Academy. I really like the way you teach things and the way you explain things. So once again thank you for everything. ~Nick L.

Dear Mrs. Klinkerman,
I loved the book you had us read. I didn't think I could love another book besides <u>The Hunger Games</u>, but you showed me a book even better! I feel like you made me want to keep reading, something I haven't felt in a while, so I thank you for opening up my eyes to a good book that I loved reading. ~ Kryston O.

Thanks to you I have improved on not only my writing skills but also my reading skills. That means so much to me because those were my two worst subjects. You are so sweet and always helpful! ~Caitlin B.

Boss K,
I thank you for so much. As hard as it is for me to take your class, you have shown me a different approach to a topic I am not very good at. This has given me hope and a will to fight for my future again. Every day I sit here and work so hard running from my past and the horrible schools I've been to. The game Caught Ya' I have turned to in every assignment I do, and so you have helped me find a side of school I never thought I would find. Success. ~Devon G.

Klink,
You're a tough teacher, but I know you care about us. Thank you for pushing us so hard. ~Yanomy R.

Go, me! (If you don't have your own "Go, me!" file, I highly suggest starting one. You don't even have to publish it.)

It is a seemingly small victory for a teacher to receive compliments such as these, but in our world it's huge. You have just accomplished what some other teacher could not, and that is get a "reluctant learner" engaged again. Sadly, this is unrecognized in the world as a true accomplishment as we teachers are just expected to perform this miracle daily, and multiple times a day with our stimulating and wildly engaging Cirque-de-Soleil-esque lessons. But in reality, in an over-crowded classroom of 30+ kids and multiple periods, you're lucky to remember everyone's name by the end of the year.

Winter Graduation 2012 YourHub Write-Up

"Our greatest weakness lies in giving up. The most certain way to succeed is always to try just one more time." Thomas Edison. This quote is the mission statement of Eagle Academy High School, one of Douglas County School District's numerous "Options" programs.

The Winter 2012 graduates of Eagle Academy did try one more time, and succeeded January 12, 2012, by receiving their high school diploma from DCSD. The thirtieth commencement ceremony took place in Rock Canyon High School's auditorium on a chilly, snow-covered night. (Eagle Academy does not have its own building, but meets at night in the Foreign Language wing of Highlands Ranch High School.)

Assistant Superintendent Dan McMinimee and school board members Kevin Larsen, Meghann Silverthorne, and Steve Johnson were present to witness the ceremony and officially accept the class. Each graduate accepted his or her diploma as a projected image of him or her and their college plans flashed on the screen above the stage.

Well over 300 audience members cheered on the graduates as they told their stories of struggles to get to where they finally stood with a diploma in hand. The thanks for the staff were plentiful as graduate after graduate expressed how grateful they were to have such a "family" at

༺ঙ༻

Eagle to help them find their way. The ceremony culminated in the newly graduated class exiting to Tupac Shakur's "Keep Ya Head Up".

Congratulations to all of the graduates on behalf of the faculty and staff at Eagle!

Chapter 19 – My Very Own Hollywood Movie

"People don't have these tidy little redemption arcs in reality the way they do in movies."
~ Diablo Cody

One of the courses I designed, English Strategies II, actually revolved around the book written by the one woman to physically walk around the world, Polly Letofsky's 3 MPH: The Adventures of One Woman's Walk Around the World. She happened to become a personal friend of mine in a round-about way (as I stumbled my way through network marketing side businesses in an attempt to supplement my income). When I found out she had completed her book about her adventures, I did some quick-on-my-feet teacher-thinking and decided this would be an awesome book to use to teach rather bland strategies such as predicting, critical reading, and vocabulary. With the blessing of my principal once again, we purchased a classroom set of the books.

"Adventure Literature" - because I hated the title English Strategies II- was launched. I would teach all those important reading skills, plus skimming, scanning, summarizing, writing, vocabulary, and critical thinking, PLUS Humanities skills such as mapping, geography, culture, and art, all in one class. My first-ever class of students took to it like ducks to water. We practiced reading strategies all over the place while students laughed over parts of the book, learned about new cultures, and reflected back on some of the absurdities of the American culture as seen through this brave woman's eyes.

As the class was focused on a book about a woman walking for nearly five years (one day shy of exactly five years), I decided a walking activity was in order. I knew the Whole Foods Market down the street was almost exactly one mile from our doors, so that became a field trip. Students were not allowed to plug in their music for the walk so they would do what happened to Ms. Letofsky as she walked – she connected with people. It would make me smile from ear to ear to see the groups form and reform again and again as students really and truly talked with each other. Sometimes another teacher would join me, other times our security guard would join us, and we would walk. The first year I will never forget as my students realized we were walking past a fire station. They asked if they could get a picture on the fire truck, and I'll be darned, they did. It was beyond heart-warming to see them all acting like little kids again.

Upon reaching our destination, I would send the kids around the store on a Scavenger Hunt to find at least 25 different items imported from around the globe. I don't think management liked it too much, but the kids did spend money there, and learn the important lesson that they needed to land a better job if they were ever going to shop at Whole Foods again. I'd say that was a pretty valuable learning experience, wouldn't you?

Headed back from Whole Foods

The Fire Truck photo.

One night as we were predicting Polly's route on the next country's map, a student declared, "This is like our very own *Freedom Writers Diary* class!" To be compared to the teacher who brought a class of "delinquents" into pretty much world fame like Erin Gruwell did was one of those heavenly teacher moments. I could die happy now. Being compared to a Hollywood story such as that, or any other teacher-y movie like *Dead Poets Society* or *Stand and Deliver* is what we secretly hold as a compliment of the highest regard. After all, everyone loves those movie teachers, right? Funny how those movie teachers never have to have parent-teacher conferences, do fire drills, go to district trainings, or receive nasty-gram emails from parents, but I digress.

The end of the year project became a designing a board game to go along with Letofsky's book, and to then contact game companies to see if we could launch it as an actual product. Years later, it is still in the works as doing a project with teenagers is a process of fits and starts, and if you can keep an astronomical amount of patience at the ready, you will succeed. (Ask me about having a student from another school illustrate my children's book, Battle of the Grandmas, sometime.)

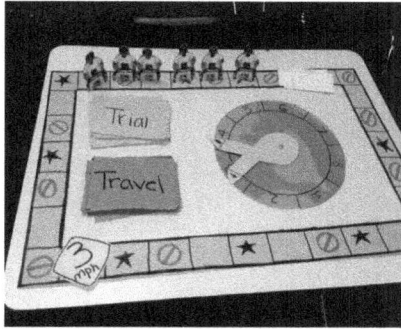

Adventure Literature student game board idea from our end of the semester project.

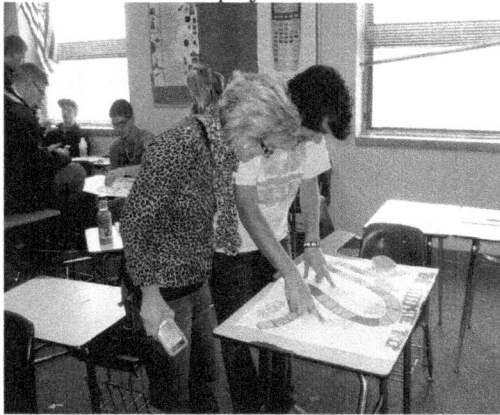

Polly checking out another game board idea.

To culminate the class, Polly Letofsky herself, a friend here in Colorado, would come in and have a meal with my students. It was a magic moment in these kids' lives, and each semester there would be a week of anticipation as we decided what food to get for the night, and what questions we would ask her. She would come in, sometimes with shirts for the kids, other times to inspect their final projects, and we would sit down like cultures do all over the world and break bread together. We ate Indian food, Middle Eastern and Greek most often as these were some of Polly's favorites, and the spices were the most foreign to the students. At the end would always be a giant group photo, and some selfies to boot.

Considering there was a time when a student asked, while moving her arm horizontally and then perpendicularly to the floor, "Does the equator go this way…or this way?", I think my Humanities class became a necessity. I'd like to believe that by semester's end, students were a little more "globally aware", which is a "World Class" outcome if I ever saw one.

As a final note here, I highly recommend getting guest speakers in the classroom at every turn. It just so happens I know the best there is.

Polly Letofsky brought shirts form her walk around the world for everyone.

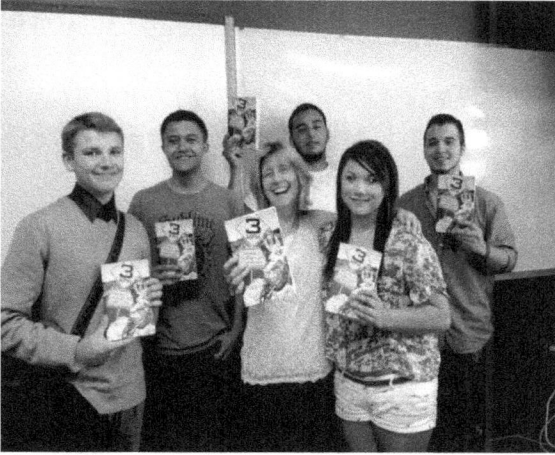

Students with Polly Letofsky and copies of her book after enjoying a tasty East Indian buffet.

The bi-annual plank competition to simulate the trials our chosen author suffered. I usually finished in the top three – not bad for someone who could be these kids' mom!

P.S - One semester's plank competition, the students were laughing that I was still up and just casually talking with them during the whole thing, as if we were out to coffee. "How are you doing that??" a mystified student asked.

Another student scoffed, "Duh! She doesn't smoke!"

෩ඥ

Chapter 20 - Tech Breaks and Other Distractions

"Technology... is a queer thing. It brings you great gifts with one hand, and it stabs you in the back with the other."
~ Carrie Snow

Technology is here to stay. Unfortunately. It is crucial to the life of a teenager, especially one who drives. I fought the good fight for years about the cell phones, even foolishly collecting them at one point because I was so tired of the distraction. The thing is when you collect them, students actually forget about them. I think it's the lack of frontal lobe development, the ability to predict they may need them later. The teacher is then stuck with a basket of cell phones at the end of the night, and in a major predicament if this night happens to be before the weekend.

Rather than assume responsibility for these little pieces of our "digital natives", I discontinued this practice and came up with the idea to give my students an actual "Tech Break". I had read something about the importance of technology to this new breed of students, and how permission to use their toys was increasingly important. The rule then became to keep them out of my sight until the five-minute break. I told them, "I respect you and your need for this kind of thing enough to even give you a break, so please respect my rules enough to keep off of the phones until then."

It was remarkably successful, to the end that the amount of "Behavior Points" I used to take away for constant cell phone-sneaking has been reduced by at least 75%. I would strongly suggest giving it a try if you have high school students, unless it goes against school policy.

The thing that always struck me as strange was how many "parent" phone calls would come in during class. "As if your parent doesn't know where you are?" I'd question. Students would assure me it was indeed their parent, and over the course of my time there, I learned that these calls really were often times parents because the parent needed something. Sometimes the family would have only one car, or need to talk with the student about a home situation, and even then I'd have to keep biting my tongue. I probably should have gone ahead and pierced my tongue for all the holes I put in it every time I'd come to this disturbing realization: here was a student trying to better themselves by finishing high school, but yet were being distracted by their own parent.

In Their Own Words:

Graduating high school is not an accomplishment, it's something that gets done. How? Doesn't matter. You are put through school to graduate, and what you choose to do after is your choice.

Eagle Academy isn't just a high school. It's a school where you meet unique personalities, hear different stories, and can relate to one another and not be judged by peers and teachers. That's a big one. In a school with 3,000 students every teacher can't take the time to know each and every one of their students. They really only get to know the talkers and the troublemakers in class. Not the student that carries their books wearing the same ripped dirty shirt, or the quiet one who is honestly struggling. This school is everyone's second chance by choice. Everyone's goal is to graduate! With the help of the kind hearts of the teachers and staff, and the positivity from students pushes each and every one of us to reach that one goal we share. I've had a hard time in high school. I started skipping class and falling behind. That wasn't what I wanted to do, I knew skipping class would lead to giving up. I don't like giving up. But it seemed way easier than dealing with a teacher that doesn't care and a peer that laughs at you for being quiet. They didn't know what I was feeling.

Soon enough I started falling behind and got off track with graduating. Then I found Eagle Academy. I had to beg my parents to let me go. Both of them didn't like the idea of an alternative night school; they both wanted me to be "like the other kids" and graduate with them when we all knew it wasn't going to happen [that way]. I made the choice to apply by myself. I had an interview with the principal, and he was willing to help me get back on that graduating list! When I told my parents I got accepted, but they were not happy at all. That didn't matter to me, I was ready to finish what was started with a new [environment]. It wasn't till almost the end of the school year that I realized I've been surrounding myself with the wrong people. It's hard to let go of your best friends. But they only broke me down as I tried to build them up. Those aren't the kind of people anyone wants to be surrounded by. For a while after I let my friends go and do their own thing, I kept quiet to myself. My grades started looking better, I got my work done, I understood everything in class. I even got Honor Roll! Slowly people started talking to me. I didn't mind keeping to myself, but it was nice to know people recognized me. Soon enough I started to open up to my peers and teachers. I've never felt better and more comfortable at school; I loved it! Next thing I knew I was graduating!

It's been over a year since I've graduated from Eagle Academy. I still don't call it a huge accomplishment; I believe I got done what I was supposed to get done. Except I now have lifetime relationships with some of those that has made a positive difference in my life. For that I am thankful.
~Julia B.

෨෬

Chapter 21 - The Dolphin Bracelet and Other Uncommon Gifts

"Each day provides its own gifts."
~ Marcus Aurelius

Getting gifts from students at the high school level is nearly unheard of, and from a population that would rather spend its money on cigarettes and other things, it's nonexistent. But I have received some.

The night my one year there was up, after graduation when we had gathered at the local brewery, the time came for me to go home and I found myself sobbing my way out the door. I had fallen hard in love with alternative education and having to leave it crushed me. I was so fortunate to get the offer to stay on their preferred substitute list.

While I wasn't called too often, I was there at least a few times a month. One night it got out that I had been a bit of a "Club Kid". Partially shaved underside of the back of my head, but still nothing like what one may think. Yes, I went to raves and stayed out all night long before these students were a spark of energy in the universe. My drug of choice was Diet Coke. Real exciting, right? Harder stuff was available, but my control-freak tendencies didn't jibe with out-of-control feelings. Sticking with highly caffeinated beverages worked better for me, my life, my fear of my lawyer dad- a whole other book right there- and my friends who needed to be looked after.

Letting the Eagle kids believe what they wanted to believe about my club days was just fine as it earned me some "street cred". And it allowed me to assure them that one still, usually, turns out okay after their sometimes indiscriminate youth.

So the night a student who was heavily involved in the club scene, jangling multiple piercings and bracelets, learned that about me, he sought me out. He gave me some props for the life, and then felt compelled to gift me one of this bracelets. Lacing his fingers with mine, he slipped the plastic dolphin-beaded bracelet from his wrist over to my wrist. "Always connected in good karma," he said. And when I looked, the other beads on the bracelet spelled out "Good karma". It was a weird moment, and no doubt the student was under the influence of something at the time, but it was like being accepted into the fold, gaining trust from the tribe. This made my subbing nights there all that much easier. I still have it hanging from a magnet on my whiteboard.

The bracelet is now a constant reminder of that sense of belonging student after student has stated they felt at Eagle. They found their wolf pack. I know that doesn't really fit with the whole Eagle theme of flying solo as eagles aren't flocking birds. But in a way that is hard to explain, though alternative education kids want to stand out, they also want that innate sense of being part of something bigger. This is simply human nature. Tattoos, piercings, and whatever else, rarely is it the case that a person desires to be a complete outcast. Music and art unites most of these kinds of kids, and it was no truer than at Eagle.

Beside that gift, I received a paper crane made from a Post-it note from a student, a drawing, and one time a Christmas gift of Celine Dione perfume. But really that was about it. Not that a teacher lives for gifts, and the haul my husband would bring home from his middle school would more than cover any of my Starbucks cravings. It is simply that at the high school age level, authority is something to be bucked, and a student is certainly not going to admit even the slightest inkling of fondness of a teacher by purchasing a gift for said teacher. That would go against the grain of all things cool.

Another student took a liking to my paisley lanyard from a big box store. He kept offering to trade me for it, mostly to distract me from being all over his case for constantly being distracted in class by his phone. I caved in, and traded him for his "GLMR KLLRS" lanyard. I still don't even know who these people are.

A teachers-only game called "WTF", or "Witty, Thoughtful Friend" was akin to Secret Santa all year long. You would be assigned a secret friend to provide goodies for, from favorite magazines to, naturally, chocolates. It was morale-boosting to get a little surprise in your mailbox each month when your WTF could play. (Mine one year missed about two months, but to her credit she was out on maternity leave. I received a great glasses set after that!) Gifts from the principal were another thing I looked forward to because our Christmas goodie bags every year would contain delightful collections of funky Christmas music. He would burn copies of for each of us, and his wife would make biscotti, and he would pack the bags full.

We had a counselor who was the Queen of Treats. She had a knack for creating gorgeous platters of healthy snacks for us, overloaded with almonds, goat cheese, berries, dark chocolate, and crackers. One Teacher Appreciation Day she tried her best to make our dismal staff lounge a respite, a spa-haven for us, complete with candles and table cloths, and soft music playing. It worked. We didn't want to leave when it was time to go to class. We needed the "soul-fueling" because it was a known fact our sanctuary could turn into a triage unit in a heart-beat.

ഇ⊙ಬ

Chapter 22 - You've Never Seen a Graduation Until...

"I just want to show the world it's never too late to get your diploma, and show kids they should stay in school and not wait until you're old to get it."
~ Flavor Flav

Graduation is an entire chapter unto itself. During my tenure at Eagle, we moved the location three times. In the good old days, we celebrated the commencement at the Douglas County Fairgrounds in one of the larger halls. There was a semi-trailer that opened up into a stage that was driven into the hall. It really looked like a giant tanning bed with its rows of fluorescent tube lighting, but it worked.

As is the case with any ceremony, there has to be a hitch. Besides the standard technology failures during a public presentation, some of the more notable gaffes included the times we had students insist on singing a song in front of the entire audience. There was the wild student guitar solo, him playing with his long hair whipping around as though we were at a heavy metal festival. Then there was the time our principal's cell phone rang in the middle of his speech, the time a would-be streaker was caught before the ceremony started, and the time we had to start 25 minutes behind schedule because the presiding school board member was lost and couldn't find the school.

Dinner was part of the evening, and when we still held graduation down at the fairgrounds, we would take the graduate class of 22 or so to a little Mexican restaurant around the corner. Each staff member would choose a couple of students to say a few words about over dinner, but the practice was dropped because of the prevailing sentiments that some students were receiving more attention than others.

At rehearsal, the senior-most staff member would deliver a speech cautioning the kids about their two minutes at the microphone. They each would get a chance after receiving their diploma to say whatever they wanted, with the exception of any "F-you, Mr. So-and-So; I did it!"s as we were trying to keep this classy in front of all the school district honchos.

After that he would give a rather chilling reminder about the kids celebrating responsibly. The message was clear, but he would drive the point home by telling the soon-to-be-graduates, "I don't want to be celebrating your success this week, and then going to your funeral next week."

Legend has it there was an officer of the law at one graduation, waiting patiently for the student to receive his diploma so he could arrest him shortly thereafter. Another teacher saw one of our more notables pulled over already shortly after the ceremony. Still another time a student was so stoned during the ceremony (again realized too late) he broke into song during his speech to sing Van Halen's "Hot for Teacher" to one of our younger female staff members.

Still, graduation was something to behold as often I was told a student was the first one to graduate from high school in his or her family. As appalling as that was for me to hear, to see their beaming faces during their two minutes at the microphone made it all better. These students were getting a taste of the success that had eluded them for so long in school. It is a bold-faced reminder that not everyone's journey through school is the same, and not everyone's journey is full of sports, social clubs, and cheerleading. There were no letterman's jackets there, no lockers, no woodshop or art classes, no Consumer Family Science classes, not even an actual cafeteria. But it worked. For kids who needed the alternative program in order to get the basics and get out, it worked.

Winter Class of 2015

ഌരു

Chapter 23 - Art and Talent Make a Showing

"Art is an expression of who we are, what we believe, and what we dream about."
~ Julianne Moore

Even though we did not have an art class, there was plenty of talent in the school. As I mentioned, the art on student folders was extraordinary, and it often pained me to throw them out when they were left at the end of the year. A former teacher organized an annual art/talent show for our students to participate in and show off their talents at the end of the year. Students could display their art, or photograph, or perform musical or written pieces.

It was truly awe-inspiring to watch as nervous students got up to perform their talent in front of their peers, something they had never been given the opportunity to do. Even staff members could get up and share, and in the span of two art shows, I took my children's book from manuscript to the real deal. Safe expression for staff and student alike is tantamount for a successful school like this.

One particularly astonishing show, student after student became inspired to get up, to the point the evening went over regular school hours by 20 minutes. And still the audience sat respectfully and supportively as each student overcame their fears and shared his or her "gifts" with their friends. It was pure magic that enveloped the room that night.

The last one I attended, as it became an annual tradition, was as breath-taking as the first. A Native American staff member got up and sang for the students. It was a hauntingly beautiful honor song to lift spirits of protection around them as they approached the end of their schooling. The very hairs on my neck stood up – the moment couldn't have been more symbolic. Our "warriors", some fighting inner demons and some who fought even us every step of the way, were going out into the world to do battle, to survive on their own.

A painting by one of my formers, gifted to me and now holding a prominent place in my day school classroom.

A project my seniors did was designing their own logos highlighting what they value and know about themselves, and writing an accompanying essay. Here are just a few.

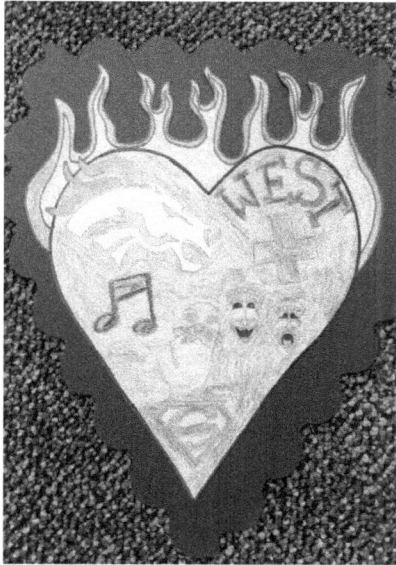

Another Senior logo. Obviously a Broncos fan.

ക്ര

Chapter 24 – The End Was Near

*"To do what you wanna do, to leave a mark - in a way that you think
is important and lasting - that's a life well-lived."*
~ Laurene Powell Jobs

It was my birthday week again and my WTF (Witty Thoughtful
Friend.) had given me flowers. I was leaving the building as I was still
part-time then, carrying all my bags and the flowers downstairs when the
principal came out and offered to help. I agreed, but when we walked
downstairs, he went to unlock a classroom and said, "Let's go in here
and talk a minute."

It was during a time of particularly great tension in the school
district, and I grew panicky. I blurted, "I'm getting fired, aren't I?"

He chuckled and said, "No, you are not getting fired."

We pushed two desks together and sat down. He said he felt he had
reached the point where the school was running itself pretty much
without him and that he felt it was time for him to seek new
opportunities. He would be the principal of a new school, out of the
district, and closer to his house in downtown Denver.

The tears started; mine, not his. And of course there was no tissue
to be found in the classroom. Stupid budget cuts. I had never had the
same boss for as long as I had had him as my boss. I was sad for me, sad
to lose him, and rightfully afraid of the building-level and district-level
changes to come, but I wished him well, then cried all the way home. He
had told me first since I was leaving, and he was planning on making the
announcement at the end of the other school night.

As it happens when one leaves the tiny nest of a tight-knit staff,
people want to protect themselves and to that point begin distancing
themselves from the person leaving. I watched as this happened even to
our beloved principal. I found him alone in our dining room/work hovel
one night, and he said remorsefully, "I guess I scared everyone off."

The time came to start looking for a new principal, and I was
darned sure to get in on that committee as I wanted a say in who was

going to take the helm of this ship. We set up the process to include both staff and students, although experience had taught me this is more for show than actual input. As long as the people at the district level like the candidate, the rest of it is out of anyone's control. In came a candidate who could talk the district talk and walk the district walk, and I recognized it during the interview. I recall leaning over and saying so to a colleague as the candidate was personally escorted out by a district-level presence. "That's who we're gonna get," I said.

And we did.

I held on for another two years under the leadership of what felt like the polar opposite of my beloved boss. Not every boss is perfect, and he may have been a little lax at times, but personally I'd prefer to work for someone with a sense of humor, and a real feel for the type of work alternative education teachers do. The new principal had begun a program in Nebraska for alternative ed, but it was apparent he was not prepared for our "clientele" that first year. Trying to rule alternative kids with an iron first is only going to earn one quite a few enemies, and predictably the kids fought back. We had more drug incidents and theft than we ever had in all my years at Eagle. Students blatantly ignored him as he yelled at them in the hallways, even ran away from him when he gave chase to students skipping out or about to be questioned for substance abuse.

As I said, I held on for two more years, and ultimately returned to teaching in a day middle school. This may discount everything I have said about being an alternative education teacher in a reader's eyes, but being a good teacher also includes knowing when it's time to put your family first, and when it's time for a change of venue.

I got tired. I'll admit it. I think those who have hung in the longest have done so because they are simply different people than I am. The Curmudgeon, J, is a male, and let's face it: most males don't have near the child-rearing responsibilities most females do. He has even said the reason his marriage is going on 18 years is because he and his wife (a day teacher) don't actually see each other until summer.

The other "lifer", Doc, is the consummate mother-figure. The kids even called her Mama R., and she called them her "babies" in return.

Her outside life family gatherings are nearly always 30+ people, and I admire her for it all. During this past graduation of Spring 2016, the first graduation I could not actually attend due to travel for a family member's graduation, she and J were presented with plaques to commemorate all the time they devoted to Eagle. (I watched the live stream.) Actually, the engravings included their families, too, as the time devoted to a night school is time away from one's own family. Rarely is there balance, but you know what they say about risk and reward.

Spring Graduation 2011 YourHub Write-Up
    It was a little difficult to determine who was more excited for graduation, the graduates or the audience at Eagle Academy's second largest commencement in the school's 15-year history. The evening of May 26 brought more than 300 family members and friends to witness 45 graduates walk across the stage.
    Douglas County School District superintendent and board members stood to present diplomas alongside principal Doug Seligman. Each student had two minutes to speak of their journey to that point, and almost all of the speeches included special thanks to parents and to the faculty and staff of Eagle Academy. One student gave kudos to retiring English teacher Jayne Cooper, saying, "I haven't picked up a book to read for fun since the Fourth grade. You made me love reading again."
    Graduates' future plans included college, joining the military, and attending automotive school. As the former students walked out of the auditorium, tassels turned, Bob Marley's "Three Little Birds" accompanied their buoyed steps.

ಶೋಡಿ

Chapter 25 - The Last Hurrah.

"High school is a haunted house in April, when seniors act up because the end is near. Even those who hate school sometimes cling to the devil they know. And for the kids who love it, the goodbyes are hard to think about."
~ Nancy Gibbs

Graduation of spring 2015 was my final Eagle Academy commencement ceremony as a member of its staff. I was in for an emotional night; I had not even made it with dry eyes through the night before, my last night in my borrowed classroom.

I had my students arranged in their usual circle even though it was smaller than normal as seniors do not have to attend the last week. The juniors and sophomores still had to come for finals, but my policy was to have a final, then give an extra credit opportunity. The kids finished both pieces early all three class periods, but I could not bring myself to say anything profound about my departure at the end of first period. I just stood at the door and smiled my goodbyes as the students filed past. Tears were imminent behind the disbelief that the end had arrived, for me anyway.

Second period, my wildest period most top-heavy with giant personalities, did their tasks, and then turned their attention on me.

"Are you gonna miss us?"

"Why middle school? They are just as bad as we are sometimes." (Note the self-stigmatizing.)

I assured them it was going to be a different kind of "bad", but I would make it through. One student who had gone toe-to-toe with me all semester, constantly on the phone and telling me the calls were "very important" and he "had to take them", piped up. "Klink, you've got to cuss at least once; it's the last night."

I laughed. I couldn't even bring myself to do it. All eyes were on me, and I still couldn't. Believe me, I cuss plenty at home but in front of students? Never. Well, okay, one time when finally fed up with the dismal computer sharing situation, and the available computer lab I did find was not connecting to any printers.

"You'll feel better," my circle coaxed.

So here 14 pairs of eyes were on me, and it being the last night, I figured no harm, no foul. "F-ing A, I will!" (I can't even write it, but I did say it.)

The kids roared.

Part of it was the wise teacher knowing when to let the kids win. This was one of those times. The other part? Stress-relief.

By third period? Forget it. There wasn't enough tissue in the school for my unapologetic crying. (There never is, by the way. Keep sending those boxes with your kids, then more in mid-winter.)

The next evening, I drove down to our borrowed high school auditorium to rehearse student names. J, the school Curmudgeon-patriarch, surprised me earlier in the week with an offer to read the student names a last time. It was an honor the three or so times I had done it, so since I conceded the congratulations speech to the youngest teacher on the staff (who, as irony would have it, was also leaving the school but of his own accord as well), I agreed to this most significant task. It would be a fitting end.

As usually was the case, the first half hour of rehearsal was lost to trying to track down kids who were late. Some kids were dressed up already; others were going to change later. Last minute scrambling to get the slide show of the graduates and their future plans put together. My job suddenly became herding kids to the computer and editing as they finished. I had to make the fonts large enough that I could read them without my distance glasses on.

Once the kids were all collected, the boom was dropped. Two students were not there, a brother and sister who were both set to graduate that night. The brother had been in a horrific hiking accident the day before and was in critical condition in the hospital. The silence was deafening. A statement was read that the family wanted the school to move forward with the ceremony, and that if she could, the sister would be collecting her brother's diploma in his stead. The mood in the room shifted understandably to one of quiet dignity upon the recognition of the frailty of life. We would do this for him.

After a few practice runs across the stage, we had dinner of our usual catered Chik-fil-A in the high school's band room with some decorations here and there. As was customary, the principal would present a Staff Member of the Year award. I had never received one, and was expecting to be disappointed again as recognition was hard to come by it seemed. However, there's always that glimmer of hope. *Maybe since I'm leaving...?*

No, it went to our new counselor, but deservedly so as he was the one who started up the after school Frisbee games so critical to our young men, and women, who were so lacking in positive male role models. That was more than fine by me.

The mood turned somber as Doc, our matriarch, approached a stack of yearbooks. I had already learned each of the departing teachers would be getting one, but I was not anticipating a big deal. Seeing Doc looking so sad ended any ideas I had about remaining composed as we were called up one by one. Eventually there were 12 of us standing there, some stoic, some sniffling. I was one of the sniffling, and then the tears started to roll. I hugged her when she finished, then the students started coming up for their hugs. I was beyond grateful I had had the sense to put on waterproof mascara that afternoon. The last thing I had ever wanted to have happen was to have students thinking I gave up on them. Graciously, these about-to-be graduates simply hugged me quietly as they arrived at the mutual understanding that they, too, were moving on with their lives.

The time had come, after the students were admonished not to do anything stupid on their "smoke break", to get them in their caps and gowns. There were plenty of selfies being taken, as well as the one group shot I used to put in the citizen journalism paper, YourHub.com. Only a few students took photos with me and the other departing teachers, but I didn't put myself out there as much as I could have either. I'm certain we were all doing this as part of the distancing that people do when things hurt.

ॐ

When I had decided there was enough melancholy, I asked one of our "cowboys" to prove his two-step abilities. (I used to frequent country bars after my rave days ended – talk about going to extremes.) He agreed to give me a spin or two, and in the breathless twirling, I heard some impressed "Ooos" and "Ahhs" from other students watching. I heard my name and was snapped from a past place reverie. Line up time had arrived.

We headed into the hallway, teachers out front. It was getting real. The last time I'd be doing this. Proudly, I led the line down into the auditorium, being sure to reserve the farthest seat in the row for the commencement conductor, J.

All the staff turned to watch the graduates enter, and the audience exploded as they usually did. This was a "hard-fought and won" day in so many of their lives. Even in 2015, even in one of the top five wealthiest school districts in the nation, this event is still a first for some families.

The evening went by in a blur, not to gloss over the important details, but it really did. The graduation speakers all started with emotional tributes to staff, and I knew I was a goner.

Then it was time to take the stage to read the names. A bittersweet moment, to be sure. The list of names that year was one of the longest we had ever had, and fortunately for me, one of the simplest. You worry about these things, you know, because this is a big moment for these graduates, and after a lifetime of having my own name screwed up, I did not wish to do the same to these kids.

I was down to the second to the last name when it happened. That second-to-the-last student, the one who had given me grief all year long, got to the podium and thanked me directly for making my little Rants and Raves class opening the best part of his day. And in front of 300 people I started to cry. He came across the stage at me and hugged me and, as one can see on the video, it took some arm-flapping to collect myself enough to read that final name. And I gave that last name on the list all I had before my exit.

My last teary task the next day was this write-up:

ೞഩന

Eagle Academy's Spring 2015 Commencement a Bittersweet Ceremony

The night of June 4, 2015, was as bittersweet a ceremony as one could expect to witness. The graduating class of Spring 2015 was one of Eagle's largest, with 42 graduates making their way across the stage to receive a hard-earned diploma from DCSD. The absence of one graduate, who was in a serious hiking accident the day before, weighed heavily on the hearts and minds of the tight-knit class, and many struggled with emotions as the student's sister accepted her diploma, then his diploma on his behalf.

Also lending to the emotions was the imminent departure of 12 long-time staff members. Still, the ceremony contained laughter and light moments before the crowd of nearly 500. As each student received their diploma, they had two minutes at the microphone to say a few words. There were shout-outs to every staff member, moms and dads, family members, and significant others, and even one rousing rendition of "Happy Birthday" for a graduate's mom. Graduates received cheers and applause in return.

As is tradition, the graduates chose the recessional song, the aptly titled "Bright Side" by the KnowMads. Many parents and grandparents at the reception remarked it was the most heart-felt ceremony they had ever seen; one grandfather said to this staff member it was even better than his own graduation.

Congratulations, Eagle Academy Spring Class of 2015! You will move the world!

My Very First Commencement Speech- Winter 2009

There are so many clichés I could have started with, but the long and short of it is Eagle Academy fits. I was thinking Goldilocks and her "just right" chair and porridge, the old "Square Peg/Round hole" cliché,

97

the glass slipper metaphor, clear to the Native American saying, "To know another man walk a mile in his moccasins." But Eagle Academy is anything but a cliché or a proverb, so I thought I'd start with a story instead. Aren't most stories about fitting in anyway?

So boys and girls, ladies and gentlemen, once upon a time, there was an idea. It was an idea for a much needed place for students who didn't quite fit the day school model. As irony would have it, this school had to fit into another school. So it tucked itself into another high school's halls, nestled into its corners, and seeped into its desks and became Eagle Academy. Teachers and staff came and discovered that they fit in with this idea of a school, and they opened their minds and hearts to let Eagle sink in there, too. Students came along, and they were absorbed by the idea of this safe place where they found they, too, fit in nicely.

These students discovered they were not expected to be one thing or another… they were just expected to be. The teachers found they were just expected to offer each student encouragement and success in whatever form it chose to take.

The faculty watched and waited, and one year grew to two, then four, finally a decade. And the students came, and they graduated, and they returned to catch up with the staff that they knew wanted more than anything to see them on this stage, no matter what it took. One particular staff member threatens to "love kids across the finish line or kick them across"; that was their choice, but it was their ONLY choice. Parents, you may have said something very similar at one point.

Obviously, they made the right one, or you now know why graduation gowns are long.

I owe this story to a discussion we had one night in my class about "good" schools and "bad" schools. The realization came that there really aren't good or bad schools. There are simply places in which we don't fit. I personally found getting up at 5:00 in the morning to teach at day school to be REALLY inconvenient. Luckily for all of us, the place where we do fit was right around the corner, offering a different experience, a different way of accomplishing a common goal.

Like puzzle pieces jammed into the wrong places, our students, some of us teachers, maybe even the principal, came here a little frayed and bent around the edges. As time went on, however, the edges smoothed out and the pieces fit together to create a bigger picture.

So, whichever way these graduates came to be here today, they found their glass slipper, their "just right" fit. Only now they leave a student-shaped hole in the hearts of Eagle Academy, and their families, too, as they head off for their next adventures.

Whether it's their next school, their career, their relationships, their lives, may they always have the wisdom to recognize a good fit. They already did it once, and now they wear the caps and gowns to prove it. Here is wishing the January 2009 graduates of Eagle Academy continue to find their fit.

Winter Graduation 2010 YourHub Write-Up

Thursday, January 14, thirty-one students walked across the stage at Castle View High School to accept their high school diplomas. There were hoots and cheers, an air horn, and cries of "I love you!" from the jubilant audience, as well as tears and heartfelt speeches from the graduates on stage. Each student's picture was projected onto the screen overhead, accompanied by a short biography about where the student was planning to enroll after graduation. Several teachers dabbed at their eyes as students recognized them and all of their efforts, and plenty of people choked up when a student called out, "I'm going to make you proud, momma!"

From all of the faculty and staff at Eagle Academy, congratulations to each and every one of the Eagle Academy Winter 2010 Graduates.

Waiting to get the party started!

Spring 2011 Congratulations Speech:

I have a confession to make – I "cribbed" part of my speech! It was just too good to pass up.

I had a friend getting ready to travel the world. Her mom stood at the starting line and delivered this speech: "I know you are traveling light, but there are a few things you should take along. Take patience. You will need it on long desolate stretches and busy border crossings. Take an open mind to let in new and strange experiences and see the good, the amusing, and the beautiful there. Include a good supply of courage. And don't forget wisdom. Strap it to the top of your pack. You will need it every day."

Now you know I love a good metaphor, so I'm borrowing this one. You are standing at the starting line, ready to head off on your own journey. The whole world lays in wait at your feet. Along with everything already mentioned on the packing list, I will recommend three more things.

1. Take along the knowledge that you matter to everyone you meet.

2. Take trust. You have made it this far, and will make it farther still. The depth of your past is in no way an indication of the height of your future.

3. Take heart. You are standing at a border crossing right now, and everyone is watching you head off into your future, and rooting for your success. Well, FORMER students, we're handing you your "passport" and sending you on your way. Congratulations, Eagle Academy Spring Class of 2011!

Best graduation speech from a student ever:

The "Dear Mr. Vernon" essay from The Breakfast Club. (See Chapter Three.) Coming from a student who NEVER spoke, it took all my restraint to not stand up and cheer. I may have let out a "YEESSSS!!" though.

Spring Graduation 2013 YourHub Write-Up

Some impressive numbers occurred the night of June 6, 2013. Thirty-five graduates. Thirty-third commencement for Eagle Academy Night High School. Twenty-three staff members. Over 500 friends and family. A second chance culminating in one hard-earned diploma.

This was a bittersweet gathering as it was the last graduation ceremony for departing principal Doug Seligman, and three other staff members. However, it was also the birthday of senior Jacob P., and his fellow graduates led the audience in song to wish him well. Three students, Matt D., Keaton L., and Cameron W. are joining the military in the near future and were given a standing ovation.

Earlier in the evening, as tradition goes, students were given a private showing of a farewell video they had helped to create. Much to their surprise and delight at the end, faculty and staff had earlier recorded their own version of "The Harlem Shake".

Tears were plentiful as the crowd spilled out into the warm night, and cameras snapped everywhere as new futures began. Congratulations, graduates!

Graduating class of Winter 2014

Winter Graduation 2015 YourHub Write-Up

    The Class of January 2015 wasn't even around to have been able to see the "The Breakfast Club" in theaters, but there were plenty of references to the great 80s teen-coming-of-age movie at the commencement ceremony on January 15, 2015 at Rock Canyon High School.

    From the recessional song, "Don't You Forget About Me" by Simple Minds, to a student who surprised everyone with his two minutes at the microphone by starting, "Dear Mr. Vernon..." Student Max Stakely read the notable movie essay in its entirety, in it contained a poignant reminder that kids will live up to are what they are labeled. Fortunately, this class shook off all their previous labels to become "high school graduates".

    Congratulations to the Eagle Academy graduates! We are expecting great things from you, and we certainly won't forget you!

Chapter 26 – Some Odds n' Ends n' Free Food

"Our whole life is solving puzzles."
~ Erno Rubik

If you don't like having multiple "preps", that is, preparations for multiple classes, education is not for you. From elementary to college, a teacher doesn't just get to teach the same class over and over multiple times a day. Or night. And explaining the nuances of a classroom to a substitute? Forget it. Again, that's why most teachers will come to school on his or her death-bed because the efforts to explain it all in sub-plans are monumental. Here is a just a sample, and you are certainly not expected to read all of it.

Sub Plans – *Keep in mind this is ONE NIGHT, but one very important family night for me:*

Sept. 19, 2012

Dear Substitute:
Thank you so much for taking my classes tonight. It's my daughter's 9th birthday and she did not want me to miss out.

In my cabinet, you will find all the kids' folders in black stand-up crates on the top shelf. The only one not labeled is my Period 3 class. Pull those out and set on front row desks, along with my supply "tin", and the small black crate with my bathroom pass (Snoopy lunchbox) in it. (There is lined paper on top of that – they will need that out, too.)

Period 1 3:15 – 5:00 English Strategies II

Class text – Miss Peregrine's Home for Peculiar Children. Each student put a post-it note on the cover to keep track of their pages now that they are reading independently. Have them read for 45 minutes.
Then give the vocabulary exercise – the dictionaries are on the top shelf of my cabinet. Give then another 30 minutes to do this, then go over their

---

definition with them so whatever they chose to use (phones are okay for this exercise) they all have similar definitions.
Please collect vocab work and put in my mailbox at the end of the evening.

Period 2 5:00 – 6:45 Grammar & Composition

The kids are to come in and get started on the DOLs/Caught Ya's they have in their folders. They are to do # 19, 20, and 21. If you are comfortable, go over the corrections with them, or have a student who thinks they have all of them read the corrections out to the class. Each sentence has a vocab word or two so please have one student get a dictionary to give a working definition of the words so all students keep a running record of these. Collect #16 – 21 for the week. Please tell students that the project we started Monday we will finish next week with better technology.
Also, we put into effect a dinner-time detention on Monday, (they will need to be reminded) so any students names recorded tonight will owe me 5 minutes on Monday.

Have students each get a copy of the Scholastic Scope/Read Magazine. Have them put their names on these, on the cover, because they will be writing IN THE MAGAZINE AND RECEIVING CREDIT. Allow 45 minutes. Tell them to use pen.
Have students do all of the following activities:
    p. 2-3 "Grammar's Favorite Aliens"
    Read "Out of the Tornado" p. 4 – 9, keeping track on the paper of the bold-faced terms, and then providing a definition for each in the margins. (There are only 4.)
    Read "You Danger" pages 10 – 12. Do the "What Do You Think?" activity in the magazine, the Yes/No part, AND the Examine Points on Both Sides
    Read "The History of Yum", pages 19 – 20, then "The Making of a Candy Hit", page 21.
    Lastly, do "The Lazy Editor" activity.
Collect Magazines
(IF there is time left over, do the play p.13-17.)

Period 3 7:15 – 9:00 Dramatic Literature

This is my most fun class!! The books, <u>Nothing but The Truth</u>, are in the green district bag on my top shelf. Have Connor H. or Kevan S. help find them, if you need. Find the copy with the yellow sticky-note bookmark – this is where we left off Monday. The kids are AWESOME at voices and reading, even acting out scenes if you are comfortable with that, so all you need to do is prompt them for the next scene. Read for 45 minutes.

Give them a 2-minute stretch break. When they return, read to them the article I cut from the paper today. (Some of the characters are reporters, and the students are now getting a feel for how newspapers slant stories, and how reporters are not always accurate.) Have them focus on the highlighted paragraph, then have them write a ½ page response to that statement as it applies to the three journalists/reporters (including the radio Talk Show Host, Jake Barlow) in <u>Nothing but the Truth</u>. Collect.

Continue reading out the play for the rest of the class period, and please mark where you stop. There are some really awesome discussions that begin in this class, and you should have a terrific finish to your evening! Thank you so much!!!

<u>Comment added upon reread while editing book:</u>
Holy h*ll, right?

Another honor a high school teacher gets is writing letters of recommendation for a student furthering their educational endeavors. Knowing college is not on the immediate horizon for many of the students in an alternative education setting, you get an enormous thrill when asked to write such a letter, even many years past graduation. Here is one such letter:

<u>Student Recommendation Letter:</u>

Colorado Mesa University

January 21, 2013

Dear Colorado Mesa University,
    I am writing to recommend a student for your academic institution. Hayden B. has been in my Grammar and Composition class for the past

semester, and he has shown an affinity for getting across intelligent points in his essays.

Not only that but he demonstrates a genuine interest in getting correct answers when editing grammatical mistakes; a rarity indeed! He shows the initiative to rely upon himself and not spell-check or other tools at his disposal, and as a matter of fact was the only student to take me up on the offer of providing a list of alternative transition words to aide in his essay projects.

On a personal note, having students show this kind of gumption when temptations are huge to "borrow" unoriginal ideas on the Internet is refreshing.

For this reason, in particular, added to his ability to make a solid point in his written communications, I am happy to recommend Hayden B. to be an exceptional addition to Colorado Mesa University's vibrant student body.

Sincerely,

Anthonette K Klinkerman
English Literature
Eagle Academy High School

Being in "The Most Interesting District in America?" (Question mark added by the authors of the article, not me, though tempted.) by Frederick M. Hess and Max Eden, the criteria for keeping your job now includes some rather strange business-world techniques. (It's not working, and to date no one has done any "'splaining.") Market-based pay, evaluation systems that could confuse Einstein, and a site to which we must upload "evidence" that proves we aren't sleeping, let alone sitting, at our desks all day, in addition to being observed twice a year by our administrators. One can pretty much determine why the district has lost so many fine principals and teachers over the last five years as no one has time for all of this paperwork on top of actually teaching. I've included below an actual observation from a time when one live professional sat in a classroom and watched a live professional in order to provide honest and human, not algorhythm-produced, feedback.

ഇരുന്ന

When Teacher Evaluations Were Simple:

> Eagle Academy Formal Observation (from D. Seligman)
> Teacher: Anthonette Klinkerman
>
> Pre-Observation Conference Date: 3/12/13
>
> Classroom Observation Notes: Agenda on Board
> The students and teacher were discussing gender roles and stereotyping. Anthonette clarified student statements for the entire class to hear. Then she explained the directions for the follow-up activity. Two students read aloud from the book to provide examples of stereotyping in the novel. Anthonette assisted with some unfamiliar vocabulary. Students formed groups, collected materials, and started the project. Anthonette re-explained directions for some students who were confused. One group took several minutes to get started. After fifteen minutes, the groups sent to the front of the class, one by one, to share their responses. Anthonette shared a recent news story about a community in Pakistan that had been burned down because of stereotyping.
>
> Evidence of Student Learning: Students were able to insert different words in order to change the tone of the sentences.
>
> Things That Worked Well: Your expectations for the activity were very clear. Student behavior reflect prior expectations.
>
> Things to Fine Tune: Might this have been a great opportunity to have students complete a Quick Paragraph (TS (Topic Sentence), three support sentences, CS (Concluding Sentence)) to talk about the author's use of language in that particular section of the novel?
>
> Final Thoughts: How do you ensure participation of all students when reading aloud? How difficult was it to navigate the language of the novel with your students? What is your thinking around student grouping? You had the students take out the gender-biased language and insert words with the opposite tone. What did the students take away from that lesson?

Sigh. Those were the days... And those kinds of evaluations meant far more to me as a respected professional than the ones I get these days.

ഇരുൽ

Evaluations now are needlessly complicated, overly repetitive, and micromanaged down to six and seven categories for the five to six gradients. From all of that, a teacher is categorized as *Highly Effective*, *Effective*, *Partially Effective*, or *Ineffective*. You get these by having an administrator check over all your uploaded evidence for each category and subcategory, and observing you maybe twice a year. I'm proud to say I have now been spectacularly *Effective* for the last three years. Truthfully, this reminds me of a woman saying they are "sort of" pregnant. Uh, you ARE, or you AREN'T. Educators, you know this - you've got it, or you don't.

To make matters worse, each and every year we teachers, since we have all the time in the world, are encouraged to video ourselves teaching, and then watch it to write up a reflection about it. Ick, and double-ick. But here is one I did begrudgingly. I only include it now to illustrate that I DO reflect on my teaching, and I DO know what I am doing on occasion:

<u>Video Reflection of my Teaching:</u>
Teaching Video #1 Reflection (2013)

Let me start by saying I hate watching myself on video.
Ok, that out of the way, the lesson I was teaching was the standard lesson I begin each day with – revisions on paper of a short, humorous story. I use this time to walk around and help students in a more one to one way as this class is Grammar and Composition, something it is clear most struggle with. The goals of these lessons are:
Settling into the day (Bell work)
Reviewing spelling
Reviewing grammar
Listening
Writing
Vocabulary
Mechanics of writing dialogue
Teaching Irony/Humor
Penmanship/committing resolving errors to muscle memory

I have many very large personalities in this class, as you see on the video. One in particular cannot start her day without being as disruptive as possible, when others get straight to work. I have come to accept this as part of her personality, and I do not react (much) as the more attention she gets the more disruptive she becomes. (I have learned this from the past six weeks, so I just let her get it out of her system and then settle down to work.)

I cannot hear the audio that well, but I know I was giving a lot of positive feedback to students as they asked questions regarding spelling and mechanics of the piece.

The lesson combines direct instruction and one to one instruction, as at the end as a class we go over all of the corrections together, as seen on the second video. This brings in the listening part of any good Language Arts lesson, as students can be very successful on an assignment if they are focused and concerned about hearing the corrections and transferring them to their own papers. Some students still struggle with this, and I am working on a resolution.

I think I demonstrate the kind of interactions necessary for at-risk students to feel successful in a classroom where the subject matter is not their favorite, and is something they struggle with, as stated. Because this class (2nd period) always tends to be top-heavy with kids who would rather dismiss the material for socializing due to their insecurities over it, I have suggested to our counselor moving the subject matter to first period in the years to come. This would achieve a less disruptive environment for all learners as this class has historically been unsuccessful in the time slot it is in due to what I feel are two important factors – 1. students are not quite as active during first period due to biorhythms, and 2. As so many struggle with the mechanics of English, they are more likely to act out when wide awake and "stuck" on campus by second period. I would like to try this set-up for at least a year to see if my theory is correct.

(*Not to toot my own horn or anything, but it was spot-on.)

Another student perk I can't find a good spot for was the food packs. In every school district in America there are kids who don't get enough to eat, and our school district is no different. A social worker once told me that it would be surprising to most to see all the giant houses in Highlands Ranch, Colorado, that look great on the outside, but don't have a stick of furniture on the inside. The owners wanted to keep up the pretense of wealth, and having one's act together, but couldn't actually afford to furnish the house. Our kids became the object of some charity from, ironically, another high school, and their community pantry. Food packs were made – a Ziploc bag with ramen, granola bars, fruit, and other items, and distributed on Thursday nights before a weekend where some of the students may or may not have a meal until the following Monday. There was always food in our building, and always a supply of ramen at dinnertime to feed our kids before this. In fact, friend who was an alt-ed kid himself purchased a flat of ramen for the school because someone was once kind to him in such a fashion. His tears said it all as he loaded it into my trunk.

Sadly, sometimes we found the food packs thrown out, especially the fruit. Cigarettes kill the appetite, apparently.

Eventually the school gained the attention of a church group who wanted to come in and make meals for the students once a month for a community dinner. These women and men, and their children, would take over the empty cafeteria and set up the tables and food lines for things like tacos, sloppy joes, and pasta. A few kids grumbled at having to stay in for dinner on the principal's orders, others grumbled that they didn't like what was being served. But for the most part, the students were grateful not to have to spend their own money, or eat ramen for another night in a row.

The church group provided Christmas treats, even, and at graduation provided further gifts for the graduates in the form of movie tickets or Subway gift cards. I only recall one time when that fine line between church and state was crossed; there was a biblical passage in the baggies for the students. It was quickly pointed out that this was a no-no, and it never happened again. I can only hope that the students will one day pay forward such generosity.

Chapter 27 - Frequent Fliers

"You don't learn to walk by following rules. You learn by doing, and by falling over."
~ Richard Branson

As things tend to come full circle in life, I had the unique opportunity most teachers don't in that some of my students from 8th grade ended back in my classroom at Eagle. I had at least three come across my path again, and strangely just the other day I crossed the path of one of those same students.

She had been trouble since the 8th grade; combative, disassociated with the other girls, and a chip on her shoulder almost as heavy as her make-up. It was common knowledge she was in a foster home situation. She was about to get into a fight with another girl one afternoon – really just a shouting match – when the vice principal entered the room to see what all the commotion was about.

Then years later she entered my class at the night school. She was still involved heavily in drugs, and her absences became more and more frequent. She was one of those few we weren't sure was going to make it, physically. And after she left us, a few months later there was a newspaper article posting her picture among those busted in a large drug ring in the next town.

A strange measure of success, but alternative education teachers subconsciously scan newspapers and the news hoping to NOT see any of their students' faces. As if we have that much control, but that is one thing teachers always hope is that our influence will keep kids out of trouble in life.

Leaning over a counter at a thrift store, checking out the jewelry, I heard a shocked, "Mrs. Klinkerman?!"

I bolted straight up to look into my former student's face, one I had as both an eighth grader AND a senior. "Holy crap!"

I apologized profusely for my utterance as I hugged her over the counter. She then told me all about her new life; sober, married, out of trouble, in management, and working another job. She also filled me in on her brother who had attended Eagle briefly, and showed me pictures of his baby girl.

We exchanged pleasantries, and I passed her a few times throughout the store, and then I later spotted her leaving, her shift obviously done for the day. She was even carrying herself differently – assured, confident, relaxed with her place in life. Whether a teacher had anything to do with that remains to be seen, but to have her tell me at one point, "It was such a blessing to run into you today" was that heart-warming, fairy-tale ending I had hoped for. She had found her peace.

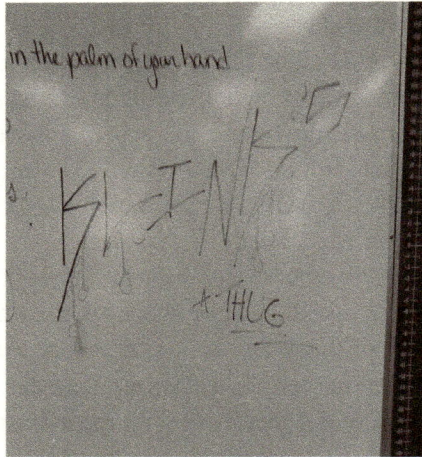

Apparently I'm a "Thug".

But at least one kid "Luhh"s me?

This was a little disparaging to walk into almost nightly. If you don't enjoy picking up after kids, teaching probably isn't for you.

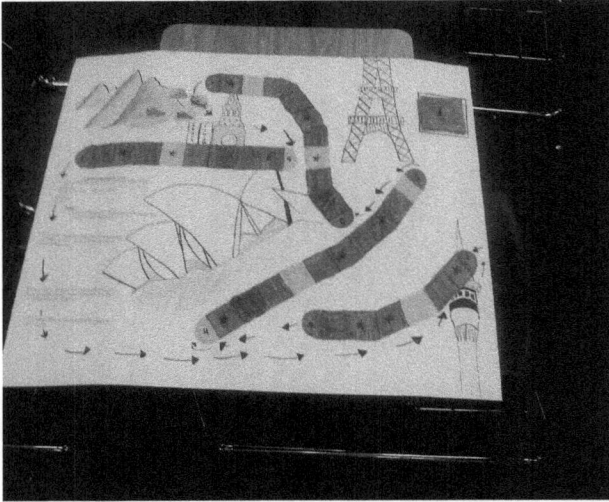

Another Game board idea for our English Strategies II book. "Adventure Literature" took on a life of its own as kids took a stroll around the globe with Polly Letofsky.

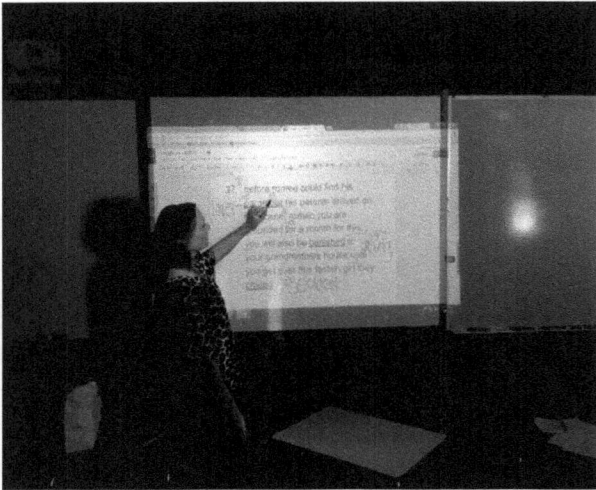

Me rarely at the Smart Board. Really, what use is it to someone who teaches reading and writing? I never could get the hang of this thing.

స෬ੴ

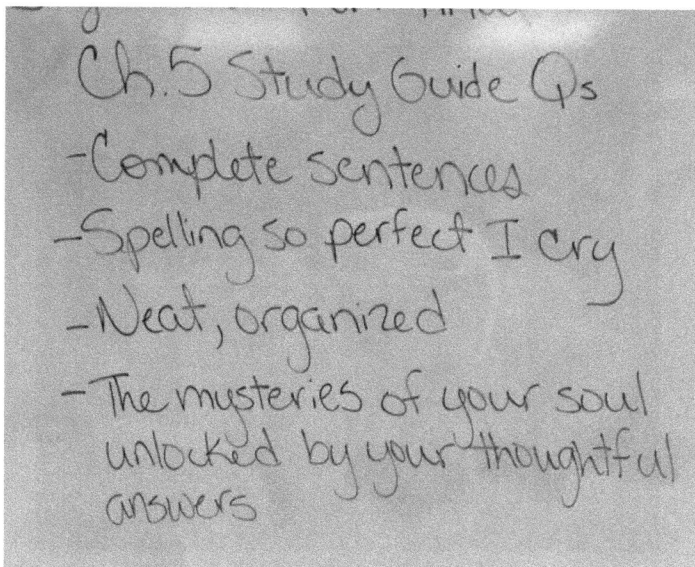

Ch.5 Study Guide Qs
- Complete sentences
- Spelling so perfect I cry
- Neat, organized
- The mysteries of your soul
unlocked by your thoughtful
answers

My expectations are high. Or, rather, "lofty".

An Ultimate Frisbee, a.k.a. "Frizz", game in progress. Who needed a PE class
when this many staff and kids were willing to run around the gym?

Outdoor Ed night was a little intimidating for some students and the counselor. Using the district's Outdoor Ed facilities in Larkspur, Colorado, students overcame fears on the High Ropes Course, and practiced teamwork early on in the year, then cooked hotdogs and made S'mores around an open fire.

A protest gathering before the school board election 2013. Parents and teachers had grown frustrated with the educational reforms being tested on their kids.

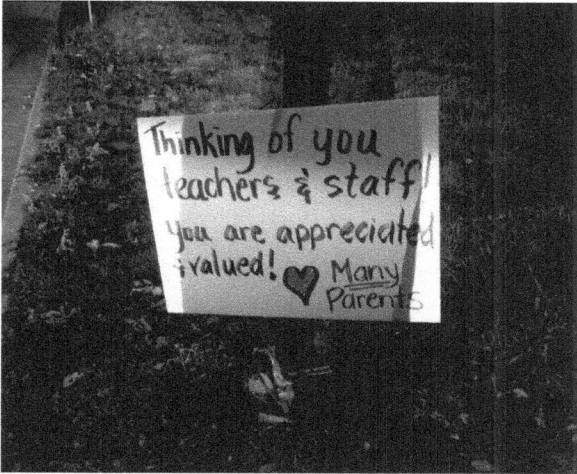

What I saw in the parking lot the night of the school board election 2013. Parent groups were pulling for a change in the leadership in the district, but did not achieve desired results until the 2015 election.

Students getting the hang of the balancing wire at Outdoor Ed night.

සිටින

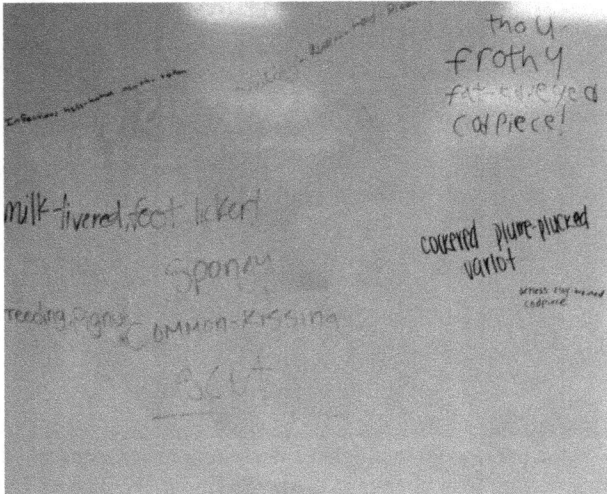

Shakespearean insults – always a favorite during my few attempts to teach The Bard.

"Frizz" (Ultimate Frisbee) became "a thing" for a lot of students. After school, 9:30 at night and music blasting, the gym was the place to be.

ℰℴℭℛ

Chapter 28 –"THAT One Student" Applies Here

"A true teacher defends his students against his own personal influences."
~Amos Bronson Alcott

My first full-time year of teaching happened to be 1999. That was the year Columbine snapped everyone out of their blissful classroom worlds and created a hyper-sensitivity to the students who skirted the fringes of regular kid behaviors. Though I was often asked when I taught at Eagle if I was afraid, I never was. In fact, I'd practically laugh at the asker of said question because I never felt safer. However, towards the end of my time there, we received a student who did fit the description of the type of student about whom we educators have been trained to be concerned. Black hair, black clothes, unusually quiet and socially restrained. I'm not going to lie – I was fearful for the first time. But so was another teacher. We shared the uneasy feeling created when he was in our rooms, and kept the office staff informed.

After the first nine weeks with us in which he rarely attended class, this student ended up on academic leave. The other teacher and myself were rather relieved, truthfully.

When the student returned to classes, though, there was something different. Something had changed. He was more engaging, and now and then I saw him smile. We had some really remarkable teachers heading up the Star Lab, so he must have made some connection with the teacher he had because he seemed ready to be a part of school again.

One evening, we were working on a writing assignment, and I had gone over to look over this student's shoulder. It registered briefly that for once he had on short sleeves and was not in his usual black hoodie. His arm rested oddly across his desk, and as I leaned over to examine his paper, he slowly rolled his arm so I could plainly see the scars. Cutting. Self-mutilation. Something not uncommon in our school. It had been reported that one of our female students had cut the word "Help" into her thigh.

∞⁙

I did not react directly, but caught his eye briefly as I advised about his writing. Later I reported to the counselor what I had seen, and the counselor asked what I thought he should do. I know that sounds like a strange question coming from a counselor, but you have to understand that many times they need to gauge from a teacher what the next step should be. Are all authorities alerted, or is it something that a visit with the counselor would appease?

"Just tell him I saw them and that I am concerned enough to go to you," I suggested as my gut-feeling was that an over-the-top intervention was going to have the opposite effect.

As the night ended, I was standing in the hall in my usual post by my classroom as the stream of students moved past. The student I had been concerned with earlier approached me with a strange smile on his face, and I knew he was aware that I had talked with the counselor about him.

It was also a look of relief if I had ever seen one. Like, *Someone noticed! Someone cares!*

"You okay, kid?" I asked cautiously, and then was caught up in a hug.

"Yeah," he said when he let go.

"Ok. You know you can always talk to me, right?" I said, still peering into his smiling face.

"Thanks, Mrs. K," he said and left.

There was never another mention of his scars, or any further intervention from the counselor that I was aware of. After that one moment, this student was even more of a positive presence in my class, telling me everything about his love of Japanese, and startling fluency in the language, and how much he enjoyed Manga (Graphic) novels.

Before he graduated, I had to tell him I was signing him up for the 180 Degree Award as I had never seen a student make such a turn-around as he did. That earned me another one of his rare smiles.

Sometimes, the biggest lesson of all in alternative education is just being the adult on a kid's side. School has been a battle almost their entire lives, and often the enemy is the adult in the room. Just knowing a teacher is on a kid's side can mean the world of difference for a student who has had nothing but negative experiences. Everyone deserves a second chance, as they say, and at Eagle, sometimes it was the seventh or eighth chance, but we still gave it to them.

Chapter 29 – Taking a Chance

"The biggest risk is not taking any risk... In a world that changing really quickly, the only strategy that is guaranteed to fail is not taking risks."
~ Mark Zuckerberg

One of the quietest students in memory had arrived at Eagle with the most unusual school picture I had seen. There was a curtain of hair brushed forward over his face and hanging down to his chin. If ever there was a societal message that this kid did not want to engage, this would have been the textbook example. A very physical shield from any and all contact, especially eye contact. Clearly a social anxiety case.

As this young man joined my classes, it took everything I had to not walk over and push his hair away from his face. But I had been around long enough to know that in due time, he would "lower the shield" himself, and until then there was nothing anyone could do about it. So we all waited. It took some time, but it happened with such suddenness it took a little while to register. There wasn't a gradual trimming back of the bangs; he just appeared one day with shorn hair, sporting glasses, and silently sat in his usual spot.

"It's nice to see your eyes," I said softly in passing, careful not to make a big deal lest I lose him. For a student with social anxiety, this was an enormous step, so drawing even further attention would have been disastrous.

Little by very little this student let us learn a scant amount about him. He was an introvert, and that's just what he was. Also a very talented writer as he would show me in his writing skills, though if you asked him to share to the whole class there was a very slim chance he would be willing.

Out of what seemed the clear blue, one evening he asked me as school dismissed if there were any writing contests I thought he should enter. This was the most conversation I had ever had from him in one

菐

stretch, so I retrieved my computer, and we sat together looking at
various young writer contests.

Doc popped in to see if I was coming along to the parking lot, saw
what was happening, and gave a wide smile. I looked up and told her,
"He's interested in writing contests so I am showing him a few." A
knowing, teacher-y smile - "Ah! Success!" - passed between us, and she
left the room. The student and I examined a few more contest pages. I
warned him to stay clear of the ones that charge money to enter, and off
he went into the night.

A year later, there he was at graduation, in cap and gown. I
returned as former staff, just to see off this group. He returned my hug
awkwardly, and I told him to keep me posted about any contests he
enters. At the microphone after receiving his diploma, his was probably
the shortest graduation speech ever: "Thank you". All of us knew this
student had just leapt over another hurdle, and that was huge.

In Her Own Words:
High school was never fun for me, I never really felt like I
belonged anywhere in high school. I always found myself in theatre[sic],
since middle school. I was hoping to get through high school with
expressing my love for that department. Unfortunately, the theatre
department at my high school was extremely cruel to me, telling me how
I'm going to end up in a jail one day, or how I'm the poster child for birth
control. My senior year I got kicked out of the theatre department
because a bunch of kids kept bullying me and making rumors about me
because I smoked cigarettes, and the department decided it wasn't worth
keeping me in it. Apparently I was too much of an embarrassment to the
the department. That's when I stopped caring about school. I started
ditching more and more classes and showing up drunk to the classes I
didn't ditch. It got to the point where I didn't show up for a two months
at all and I would drink constantly. There wasn't a time I wasn't drunk
for a majority of my senior year.

I decided to switch to Eagle because my best friend and boyfriend
at the time both attended there. As well as I had been there so many

times with my best friend who was on "academic" leave, and [went] in with him to talk to the office often. [I] was treated so differently than how my own school treated me. The first time I stepped into Eagle I felt instantly comfortable, Mr. Granat welcomed me with a compliment about my blue hair. He even told my friends who went to Eagle I should switch because I seem like a nice kid, [and] it warmed my heart that someone actually wanted me in their school. Going to school at Eagle was truly a blessing. I was so comfortable there, I didn't feel like I needed to find a place within the school because the whole community of Eagle was my place. It was right. The teachers all knew me and would joke around with me in the hall, even let me write my papers in glitter gel pens because it made me so happy. That was my favorite part. People there knew how to see the good in people. And the staff actually cared about the students, that was the coolest thing to me. I went from being shunned and shamed all the time by administration and teachers to being accepted and cared for by them. That school made me feel like a person, and like I meant something. That school gave me a reason to keep going. I was really excited to graduate on time, also frightened. I had just found a home at my school, but it was already time for me to move on. I'm glad I am where I am today, I work full time as a teacher at a private preschool. I go to college part-time for forensic psychology, I don't drink anymore, and I'm a proud mother of a puppy and a cat. Eagle helped me get to the place I am today, and I could never thank them enough.

~Cara King

ഓരു

Chapter 29 - The Lasting Effects

"We look into mirrors but we only see the effects of our times on us –
not our effects on others."
~ Pearl Bailey

One evening of summer 2015, after I had already made the painful decision to leave the night school and go back to teaching days, I received a Facebook message from a female student who had graduated in 2009. *"Hey... So I keep thinking about senior year and when you brought your wedding dress in. I'm having a super tough time And I feel like you telling me that story again will help me right now. Just reaching out because this is a horrible feeling and I need some positive reinforcement."*

I paused to recall that in that particular year, I had launched my public speaking career by recounting a moment in my life when I was very close to marrying a man who was not a good fit for me. Invitations printed, dress purchased, and everything. I kept the dress, and began telling the story to some of my women's groups. The message was that we do not have expiration dates, and that rushing to marry before 30 is not a good idea. It just so happened I told that story with the dress as my "prop" to a girls' group one night at school. This student had remembered.

I replied to give me a call, and a few minutes later my cell rang. A very teary voice on the other end greeted me. I had gathered from her recent posts that a wedding was very close, but she wasn't happy about it. She told me how she had remembered the story I told, and that her mom had encouraged her to call me. From there our conversation lasted for well over an hour, and I assured her that even though she felt like she was going to stop breathing that she was opening herself up to something so much better. An engagement is never supposed to feel so terrible. That going through with it when it feels so wrong is going to be far worse than calling it all off now.

When we had exhausted the conversation, she thanked me for being there. I actually felt I owed HER a Thank You for remembering something I had said so many years ago! She promised to keep me posted, and since that phone call we have kept in touch. She and I met for lunch one day when she wasn't working as a nanny. My former student recounted the whole story, and how much it meant for her to have me stay in touch and to talk with her when things seemed so bleak. I very nearly burst into tears at the lunch table. Watching her become all the stronger for what amounted to a 60-minute phone call, and going on with her life as I had once done, made my whole heart sing.

It's doubtful she remembers, but a few months after she had graduated, she became involved with a network marketing company, and she had asked for my support then. I had done my share of MLM (Multi-Level Marketing) companies, and I knew how much it sucked to have people turn you down, so I let her come and do her thing. And I still have a very nice set of knives to show for it.

There were quite a few times a student has called me for psychological support. For some odd reason, there was a six-month period when a number of my formers contacted me. Earlier that year, a male student who had always been on my radar seemed to be posting some rather cryptic messages on his Facebook wall. Trouble with a girlfriend, but he seemed to be spiraling out of control. I was getting very concerned and told him to call me immediately. He did, thank goodness, and we had a 45-minute conversation as I paced around the outlet mall nearby. He thanked me at the end, again for being there for him.

A few years earlier, he had had to do some detention time, and I still kept up on what he was doing. Back then he had even taken me out to lunch to thank me for not abandoning him when he needed the most support. I can't recall exactly what was said, but I had relayed that I was proud of him for "manning up" to his mistake and doing the time he deserved to do. "Man enough to do the crime; man enough to do the time," I had said, and he chuckled. Being "there" a second time for him was what I consider a gift. He had, in a way, chosen me to mentor him, and I was honored.

ॐ

Still another female student contacted me in the throes of a bad breakup that summer. I assured her that the pain was only temporary and she would be glad to be free of him soon enough. Time really does heal most wounds, and she, too, emerged better for it all.

Back to the theme of family: the fact that so many former students are still in touch, whether through the magic of social media or texting, is proof enough that there is something far more enduring happening in alternative education than in regular education. The students have found their alternative support system, and so have the teachers. If you are looking to just do your teaching job and go home, alternative education is not for you. I'm not saying that regular education teachers don't care like this, but there IS a difference. There is a certain "arm's length distance", if you will, that one can keep from their daytime students in the lower grade levels. In high school the kids can get a little closer, but in alternative education it seems there is a "forever" bond, a forever understanding that this "family" will always be there. "Once an Eagle, always an Eagle," said my principal as a few teachers moved off, and then it eventually applied to him, too. It becomes part of your heart in ways regular teaching simply can't.

Thanks to social media, once you "friend" students who have already graduated (my rule), you can still keep tabs on your family as they scatter across the globe. One is in New Zealand, one was married recently, this is one is expecting, that one is still struggling but you let him know it's going to be okay. You send her a cute meme to get her through a bad break-up. You laugh that your new hairdresser used to sit in your classroom, and now you're in *her* chair. You cry when one of them has to put down a beloved pet. You celebrate birthdays, new jobs, and a child's lost tooth. Your heart breaks when you discover one lost a relative. You smile when one is impressed with her new-found culinary skills. You fret that one has taken up rodeo. And you learn the young man who was in a serious hiking accident the day before graduation is doing just fine.

John Lennon said it best when he wrote, "And in the end, the love you take is equal to the love you make."

ၷဢၷ

Chapter 30 - Choosing the Hardest Path

"Sometimes hard decisions have to be made, and sometimes wonderful decisions have to be made. You've got to be willing to make them all."
~ Josh Homme

So why did I leave? Obviously I am profoundly infatuated with alternative education, so what made me leave? Truthfully, there were a number of contributing factors. The first and foremost was knowing my daughter was headed for rough waters as she started attending middle school. There are just some things a daddy can't handle, and frequently having to miss evening activities was wearing on my confidence as a mom. There were a few tearful phone conversations as I stood in my classroom over dinner-break when I couldn't be there to soothe a situation, and I could hardly stand the guilt. Or I couldn't stay at an afternoon function when I was part-time and I had to leave early to go to work. I'm sure it was my own conscience more than my daughter ever would hold it against me, but all of you parents know this is our deepest fear: to be told by our own children that we were a lousy parent.

The next reason was the hours were starting to kill me. Driving home late at night, especially on bad weather nights, was difficult. More so, arriving home to see the husband for a few minutes before he went to bed was tough. One doesn't just go right to bed upon reaching home as it takes a while to "come down" from being "on" as an educator. Then having to get up the next morning to do it all over again… Wake up child, feed said child, get child to school, exercise, do some of the side business, on Wednesdays pick up child at 1:00 PM (early release – the most parent-stressing concept EVER), have a snack, leave her with friends, then go to work until 9:00 PM… Those 14 – 15 hour days started to add up.

A deeper truth? I was getting weary of the drug culture some students perpetuated. I never denied it was there – it was simply more of an issue with some students than others, and watching some of the self-destructive behavior does start to wear on a soul. An interesting fact about the time warp that IS teaching: teachers get older, but the kids don't change. They will forever be the same age, still be listening to the same kinds of music, be holding on to the same category of issues year after year. The ditching class to go to some music festival or another, the getting kicked out of a parent's house, or saving money only for their next tattoo. Every year the faces changed, but some of the behaviors did not. Thankfully students graduated and matured out of those behaviors, but I started to predict behaviors still within the school walls, and I was tired.

And finally, as is true with life, Eagle started to evolve into something different. The change of principal made it into something somewhat foreign to me. A stricter, more unforgiving environment. Something I no longer felt attached to, even though I left behind some fantastic people and incredible students. The fun was gone. The district pressures to prove worth had crept in uninvited. The *feeling* in the halls was… sterilized. Distant. *Not* …me.

I went back the Monday night before Winter Break to surprise those students at their monthly community dinner, and I was overwhelmed by the love I still felt. A student burst into happy tears when she saw me, many asked me if I was going to be at graduation (I wouldn't miss it!), I received at least 30 bone-crushing hugs, including one from a student whom I had to ask to put me down. (Oh, that's another thing – full-contact hugging as I'm too short to give awkward side-arm hugs, and here no one ever got weird about it.) I was filled in on who was now class president, who was dating whom, who had dropped out, and asked more than once when I was coming back. I had had a particularly brutal week at my new school, so to have my heart refilled like that was just what I needed. Even though things were different, I missed it terribly.

Looking around at all the new faces, including all the new staff, I knew it would be hard, if not impossible, to go back. Given the opportunity to do so, I am not sure what decision I would ultimately make. I could see that the general type of student was still the same – still needing love in the worst ways. I have it to give, but the question remains, *how much would be left for my own family?* That kind of sacrifice is something many business people say they are willing to make, but then do they really take a good look at their own families to determine if they are doing what is right for them? So what if you have all the "bright shiny" in your household if you don't have the time to spend with those who are closest to you?

Time will tell. Maybe I will end up back at this wonderful place, maybe I won't. Weighing the reasons to go back to teaching days in the first place did not bring me any closer to what I would call a solid decision then, so should an opportunity present itself again, I don't have an answer. Yet. Teaching is already a give-it-all-you-got situation as I mentioned in the prologue. You either have it or you don't. But to work with those the entire system has given up on, and to set them back on their feet? Every teacher out there should do at least a year in such a setting. It changes you. You never look at a kid covered in tattoos and smoking a cigarette the same way again. And I wouldn't have it any other way.

In Their Own Words:

Well, I got to Eagle after I almost was forced to drop out of [High School] due to truancy issues. Attendance was always a huge problem for me, and because it was a public school, very few of my teachers ever tried to reach out to me and those who did only did so for disciplinary reasons. I was constantly ditching, not even to do anything really important, I just did not want to be there. For most of my life I have dealt with depression, but the last year before Eagle was rock bottom for me. I smoked, ditched constantly, and was careless and reckless in my life.

But then I found out about Eagle from my counselor at [High School], who was a huge help to me throughout my high school career. So, I ended up at Eagle when I was technically a senior, with 18 credits after three and a half years.

As soon as I walked in for my intake interview, I could see this school was different. First impressions were, honestly, caution. Everyone seemed so close, like a family, something I had never seen before in school. The students seemed like me, but they were outgoing and seemed generally happy. I didn't trust it, since my previous experiences with other students had always been cold and hostile. It was a nice change of pace but took some getting used to.

As for first impressions of the teachers, Mr. E seemed friendly but cautious as well, like he was trying to be as polite as he could be, but also thought in the back of his mind that I was sort of a degenerate. The other teachers were more laid back, and by that I mean they really seemed genuinely interested in seeing me succeed. It was strange to get used to, especially since my previous interactions with teachers usually ended up in me walking out of the class, cursing them under my breath. It was an amazing experience as time went on, and though I still had my struggles (it took a bit of time for me to transition into the Eagle family mindset), in the end I really felt like I was a part of a family. For once in my life I belonged in a community, and people liked me in it. It was very exciting, and lead to me being successful, and ultimately, graduating high school.

As for right now, I am currently living in Fort Collins and attending college for Computer Science. I have a job I love, and the friends I've made up here are amazing. Eagle taught me that I didn't have to be an outcast for the rest of my life. LOL. From my time at Eagle I learned how to be successful, and more importantly, that I COULD be successful.

~Daniel R.

꧁꧂

Chapter 31 - The Things You Don't Want to Think About

"Because I could not stop for death, He kindly stopped for me; The carriage held but just ourselves and immortality."
~ Emily Dickinson

There is a weird thing that happens in social media when there is a suicide. People make vague hints at the person's passing, or just say "RIP" and tag the person's name. No mention of causes, no mention of anything other than a few points when the writer has hung out with that person, "I'll miss you", and onto the next post.

This is how I found out New Year's Day, 2016, that a former student of mine had committed suicide on New Year's Eve. Then I did what we all do- I searched his posts for any clue, any suggestion of his suffering that I must have missed. There was nothing, but a post on December 23 where people were supposed to comment back with one word about how they had met. I didn't do it, and I regret that.

He was the kind of student that made me wonder what he was doing at Eagle Academy. Good kid, had a lot of friends, always respectful, great sense of humor. He won a scholarship at his graduation as his only goal was to head to automotive school and open his own repair shop. I followed him a bit on social media, and once we even had a brief conversation about a car I was trying to sell. He said he'd look over it for me for no charge because I was his "favorite teacher".

As I was contemplating the *whys*, the *whens*, all the other thoughts that accompany such news, I checked in on Facebook Messenger one more time. There was a three-minute-old message from another student in his class: "I am not doing well, Klink." I went into a panic, knowing how sensitive this student was and wrote back, "Call me right now, sweet one" with my phone number.

An unknown number popped up on my phone a few moments later, and I answered, questioning, "Connor?"

It was him. His voice was shaky, his stutter more pronounced that I had ever heard. Clearly he was in a state of shock. We talked for thirty minutes. I asked him where he was, whom he had seen that day, did he want me to come get him from his workplace. We laughed a bit that I couldn't possibly help him with anything math if he needed to have me help him close his workplace for the night. He said he would be okay, and he promised to call me the next day to check in.

I was beyond worried about his state of mental health after such a shock, and I told him, "You know I love you, right?"

He chuckled and said, "Yeah."

The fact that I had to think about my word choice momentarily, lest someone think something weird was going on, made me sick for a second. I love my students. Period. There. I said it. I love my students, like *any* teacher does. Not in a way that is strange or illegal; it's just something that comes naturally to all teachers. We are "fond" of our students. Even the ding-a-lings who can't stay out of trouble we harbor a soft spot for.

I waited for the call with a little fear, a little remorse. I didn't like that feeling that I left one of my "babies" to fend for himself.

The student who passed was the kind of kid who looked as though he had everything going do him- great job, a passion for cars he could continue to pursue, a loving family... It makes you wonder what could he have been experiencing that would cause such a dark solution to be the one on which he settled?

Depression takes many forms, but as we learned in the case with Robin Williams, it's often the ones with the biggest smiles who are the most depressed. This was this kid. Well, in my mind a kid as he will always be to me the age he was when he graduated. He was probably 24 or 25. In regretful recall, at a suicide prevention seminar I attended after the fact, it was reported after the age of 25, when the brain has reached its developmental completion, the suicide risks begin to decline, at least for a while. According to the American Foundation for Suicide Prevention website, "In 2014, the highest suicide rate (19.3) was among people 85 years or older. The second highest rate (19.2) occurred in those between 45 and 64 years of age. Younger groups have had consistently lower suicide rates than middle-aged and older adults. In 2014, adolescents and young adults aged 15 to 24 had a suicide rate of

11.6." Looking at the graph on the website, the age group my student was in was the second lowest line.

That day, I received a few messages of sympathy from other educators who know this pain all too well. It's always the ones who didn't fit the type who come as the biggest shock.

So is there a type of kid who harbors depression? I wish we could identify that as teachers more often, but it takes so many forms that it is impossible to produce a list that encompasses the Top Ten Signs of Depression. Sure, people try, but there are just too many. Mental health is critical, and there are too few mental health support personnel in schools. That is a given fact. There needs to be more light shed on this. Currently mental health services in my school district have a ratio of "1:925 psychologist/social worker to student ratio" and a "1:350 counselor to student ratio" according to facts released by current school board director, Anne-Marie Lemieux. (June, 2016) These numbers, though appalling, are not uncommon for school districts all over the United States, regretfully.

But I wonder, too, if this is some horrible trend in our society that more and more people are suffering from depression than ever before. I don't remember any cases like this in the high school I attended, but then it was a private school and affluent kids got into different kinds of trouble, and this was thirty years ago. Is it our water? Our food? Social media? Our struggle at basic life? I would only hope this would serve as a reminder to take mental health seriously and provide more care.

Chapter 32 – When That One Book Makes Magic Happen for a Bit

"If you are going to achieve excellence in big things, you develop the habit in little matters. Excellence is not an exception; it is a prevailing attitude."
~ Colin Powell

Cold nights remind me of the nights it would be snowing while we were at work. The kids would be pressed to the windows, practically, or they'd report how bad the roads were when they came back from dinner in hopes the principal would call for an early release. Unfortunately, the decision wasn't always his, and we would have to wait for someone at the district level to call the school and allow it. This was often a long wait as it seemed when everyone at district went home, the little night school with no building of its own was forgotten.

Often it would hit 9:00 pm with no call, so the kids would tear out of the parking lot, usually to gather at someone else's house anyway, though a few hours earlier they were panicked about "getting home". Then we teachers would troop out to the parking lot and begin warming up cars and scraping windows. Some nights we'd get out there only to find our security guard and principal had already started doing so for us. There were a few times as I let my car warm up that I grabbed my scraper and started doing other faculty cars in ankle-deep snow. It was one of the small ways we showed each other that we at least cared we all got home safely.

One of my classes, English Survey, was whatever I wanted it to be. I decided to look into a couple of young adult literature catalogues to see if there was a new book I could teacher. I found Miss Peregrine's Home for Peculiar Children by Ransom Riggs. It was too perfect: dark, creepy, and filled with photographs of weird things and people. My kids would love it; I was ready to bet money on it.

ℰℭ

Upon reading the book, I felt like I'd struck gold. This was the kind of book any alternative kid would adore as it is a "gothic novel" with delightfully dark notes.

When I presented it to my class of eight boys- by some fluke I had no girls at all in this particular class- they were intrigued. I eased into it using every book selling trick I knew: the back of the book talk, the exploration of the author's biography, the opening line that hooked me, the creepy photos. I turned them into believers by the end of the first night.

The book became a read-aloud mostly done by me, but my little book club was excited. If you can get an alternative ed kid excited about reading, you've just won the gold medal of teaching. Sure, I was doing all the work, but never let anyone tell you big kids don't like to be read to.

At the end of the first quarter, the kids begged me to order the follow up book in the trilogy, <u>Hollow City</u>. Score one for the Gipper.[1] (That means see footnote, my younger readers.)

The only drawback we had was the new kids coming at quarter. How were they going to fit into our nice cozy little book study? *I know*, I thought, *I will have two separate book groups going; the new kids on the first book, and the more seasoned kids on the second.*

Well, that worked for about five minutes. I had created an unfortunate "learned helplessness" in my gang of eight, and they couldn't move forward as strongly without my assistance. They had study questions, and I put one student in charge as they sat out in the hall, but that did not work like the teacher handbook of "freedom of choice" says it will work. (It never does.) It was a shame, truly, as I couldn't fight the system of accepting kids all through the year in order to complete a book series like this.

Tangent: To this day I lament all books that have to be some type of series. It would be nice if a book was just a book, just one part, like

---

[1] This originated in American football. Knute Rockne was the coach of the US Notre Dame team in the 1920s and George Gipp was his star player. The story goes that Gipp fell ill and when dying he asked Rockne to promise that, when things were going badly for the team, he should inspire them by asking them to 'win one for The Gipper'. (Source: The Phrase Finder)

this one is going to be. Although, J. K. Rowling? You just write whatever it is you want to write, honey. Teachers all over the world owe you a debt of gratitude for making kids readers again.

෫ඦ

Chapter 33 – Serving the Community at Large

*"There is no community service in 'Seinfeld.' But rather than lauding
that, I think it shows the insane banality of it."*
~ Jason Alexander

Students are required to have 20 hours of community service in order to graduate. Invariably, with weeks left to graduation, it would occur to students they had yet to collect ANY. So we put together some activities to help count toward the requirement. Community service nights were a bit of a joke, to be candid. Our well-intended counselor decided to make some nights where the kids did some hours with the teachers, doing things for other people.

Now it wasn't really like a canned food drive or anything, but it was amusing nonetheless to see some pretty rough-around-the-edges kids fumbling with crochet hooks, or cleaning up the trash in the parking lot, or making pillowcase dresses for African orphanages. There were some projects like making bookmarks that I wondered about, including my bright idea to make flash-card-like image posters to take to the assisted living facility down the street to help with maybe jogging memories of the patients. When I dropped off these strange- looking collages the following day, the receptionist looked at me like I was an alien. I had the best of intentions, like our counselor, but were these things really going to do any good?

The answer was actually *yes* because any community service was a service to OUR community. Getting the kids to relax and focus on a task other than school, other than a subject; to focus on each other and their teachers as people, and to have some good old fashioned, non-technology-based fun. Not to mention a feeling of selflessness, of giving of one's own time and energy. This is what community service is all about, Charlie Brown.

There was a time when we decided as a staff that we were going to have a mentoring program. A program where we each chose a number of students to really keep an eye on, to help them navigate through school and become successful individuals contributing to society. These lofty goals of any mentoring program only work when there is a connection the students have to those trying to mentor them.

What we found out in the long run was that you cannot force a mentor relationship on a student: a student must choose their own mentor. That is how it works best, if you ask for my humble opinion. What student is going to love having a veritable stranger come up and say, "Hi, I'm your mentor and you will look up to everything I do"? That would go over like the proverbial lead balloon.

Students choose whom they are going to emulate. It's pretty plain and simple. It is an honor to have a student choose you because they have done so as they somehow feel connected to you. I have had quite a few choose me over the years at Eagle, and I will readily admit that the ones I was assigned to did not remain close. Those who did called me in the middle of summer, took me out to lunch, messaged me on Facebook, but never had any initiation from me.

Case closed.

Email sent to me June 3, 2015:
Mrs. Klinkerman,

Thank you for helping me finish my high school career off in the best way possible. I truly am thankful you offer a class such as Dramatic Literature, as I grew up with a passion for theater and being placed in your class was truly fascinating and enjoyable. Your passion for literature and teaching is truly inspiring and it truly helped drive me to decide on keeping my passion in my life in the future. I completely gave up on my passion at my last high school because of the teacher's negativity, lack of drive, and inability to connect with me in a positive manner. But throughout the process of your class, I discovered my love once again and I cannot thank you enough. Not many teachers in today's society see the importance of performing arts and it was very refreshing to see you offer a class where students can discover literature of the performing arts. Your drive and dedication to the curriculum truly gave me hope and filled my last quarter of my high school experience with joy. Thank you for allowing me to participate in your class and give [sic]

ഩഽൟ

me a class to look forward to. Your passion for teaching is evident and truly inspiring. You impacted my life and made my time at Eagle truly memorable. Thank you for everything, you've inspired me to become a theatre [sic] teacher and impact kid's lives the way you did. Have a spectacular summer.

Sincerely,

Cara King

ॐ

<u>Chapter 34 – Enjoy Your Stay</u>

"No mortal man has ever served at the same time his passions and his best interests".
~ Sallust

An alternative kid does not stay in the program for long. As a matter of fact, the longer they are involved in it, the worse things seem to get. The pecking order was established every quarter. Veteran kids complained of the new kids' behavior (they forgot that at one point THEY were the new kids) because the time a student spent in the program led to a feeling of dominance over the "newbies".

Probably one of the biggest errors made at the urging of the district, most likely, was letting in younger and younger kids. The original plan was to only accommodate students in eleventh and twelfth grade, but soon we were accepting kids who were technically sophomores, and the length of a student's stay was increasing. The usual two years was now becoming closer to three, and the kids were becoming less and less focused the longer they attended Eagle.

The laments from the kids were starting to rival those of some of the teachers, including myself, when we would be sitting at dinners and saying things like, "That kid is STILL here?"

An expedited program such as Eagle needs to kept as just that, I think. The lack of sports, dances, and extracurricular subjects is for a purpose, and that is to get kids in and out of the program as quickly as possible. Why make it a place where they wanted to stay and waste time?

Then there was the self-sabotage that would occur for some students right before graduation as if they were suddenly afraid to head out into the world. Reality, when it hits, hits hard, and in all respects the quarter before a student's graduation date was the most telling. Making the decision to not turn in work or work hours to subconsciously extend their days in the safety of the nest was not unusual. It was in those moments you could see the little boy or little girl behind the tattoos and purple hair, the one suddenly afraid to come out from behind mom's legs to say hello to the world.

In Their Own Words:

My Eagle story began late in 2012. I transferred in a little early, I was coming to an end on my freshmen year beginning my sophomore year too soon. School was never my master piece. I struggled throughout elementary school and middle school and thought I tried everything. Homeschooling, online school, ditching, you name it I tried it. I gave up, I had no hope for myself and very little support from my surroundings.

When I started high school, I thought I could change. I turned into a person I never wanted to be, and within a blink of an eye; I was that person. I was ditching school, drinking, smoking, and causing havoc in my own life. I wanted to change, I just couldn't see the light at the end of the tunnel. It closed in on me, I started to believe that this person I became was who I was meant to be. I got a letter in the mail one day stating that I was going to court for not attending school. I flipped. *Could they really take me to court?* Sure as hell, they wanted to. I immediately started searching for options, and my option was Eagle Academy.

When I applied for the school, Doug Seligman, interviewed me. He asked why I should be accepted in, and what are my goals. I had no goals, aside from receiving a diploma that seemed practically impossible, I saw my life falling through the cracks. I told him everything, right then and there. Great first impression, right? Doug saw something in me, a spark, some sort of potential. I was accepted into the school and started about two weeks later.

I thought it was going to be easy, a way out of it all. But I was wrong. This school isn't for bad kids, or those of us who've made mistakes. This school was how any school in a system should work, help the student. They helped me learn, grow as person, find the path I want to walk down, they helped me become the person I was actually meant to be, not the picture I invented in my head. Eagle proves to you your own potential, and they get you to believe in yourself. I struggled still, I thought I was working so hard to graduate, I slowly started to become sober, and then I got a letter. I was on academic leave for a quarter. Academic leave was your second chance; you go to school once a week for a quarter. Now, some might think "Hey, that's pretty great". No, it was awful. I didn't get to see my friends, or be in class. I slowly started slipping through the cracks.

When I got back, it was my last semester before I graduated. And something had to change. My counselor recommended that I start going to an anonymous group in school, it wasn't so anonymous, everyone knew each other. But we respected each other, what happened in group stayed in group. Mrs. Glenn, the teacher, was a phenomenal person. She was a bright white light; her spirit would just light up the room. Everyone would explain what was going on, or ask for help. I would just sit and listen, I never spoke up much. Till one day she asked me to, it wasn't the day for it either. I came unglued in that group class. I missed dinner and my last period. Mrs. Glenn stayed by my side. She told me I could conquer my addictions, and I can grow from it. I didn't believe her, but I knew it was worth a try. I soon became completely sober, and I never felt better. Granted, it was extremely hard. I was cranky in school, almost lost my job, but I had to be honest with everyone. I came out to my teachers, and they supported me. They didn't look at me any differently or treated me like gum on the bottom of an old man's shoe. I was still a person, and a student. They would always talk to me, and the relationships I had with my teachers weren't your typical teacher-student bonding. I had real relationships with them. I loved them, they meant so much to me. They helped me get back on my feet. They supported me when no one else did, and they still do. I had three teachers that were my best friends, whether they realized it or not. Now, I'm not picking favorites 'cause all of Eagle holds a place in my heart. But these three left footprints on my heart. Dr. Rietsch, Mrs. Klinkerman, and Mr. Michalenko will forever be family to me. They taught me more about myself then I knew. They opened my eyes to new opportunities. I've been graduated for a year now, and not a day goes by where I wish I could see them. I stay in contact, always. I don't want to lose them. They are the family to me that I never got to have. If I had a car again, I'd be there every day helping out like I did when I first graduated.

When I walked across that stage and realized I accomplished graduating, I never thought about what was next. I constantly came back to school, because that was the only place I knew of. Mr. Michalenko reminded me of the speech I gave when I introduced our class. "You can't climb the ladder of success with your hands in your pockets" I wanted to keep my hands down, and stay in the place I knew the best. He encouraged me to go out and experience what the world has to offer. I quit my job, and began traveling. I traveled for almost a whole year. I went to six states, a US territory, and conquered my fear of heights. I now have a great job, I'm working hard, and I'm still living on my own. I still have my rough patches, But I always remember what Eagle taught me. Keep going, and keep your head up. The path is bumpy, but no matter what, you will always make it.

~Hannah Coghlan

ℰ𝒪ℭℛ

Chapter 35 – All-inclusive Resort, Just Not on the Beach

"So many people go through life, and they never deal with their own issues, no matter what the issues are - ours happen to be gender identity. But, how many people go through life and just waste an entire life 'cause they'd never deal with themselves to be who they are."
~ Caitlyn Jenner

We had a talk with our new counselor one night as we gathered in the hall as per usual after the "day" was done. He let us know that we would be getting a new student who was female but identified as male. We weren't really sure what to say, not due to surprise, but out of more the feeling of what we were supposed to do about it when it simply was a matter of addressing "him" correctly, and which bathroom he was going to visit. Not really a classroom/school issue as our whole motto was what is written at the Statue of Liberty's feet- "Give us your tired, your poor, your restless masses". Only at Eagle it was "Give us your absentees, your bored, your restless masses." We took them all, and we were happy to do so. We took the kids whom everyone else had given up on, put them back on their feet, and sent them on their merry way.

So this kid didn't identify with the gender they were born with; so what?

The student came to us, asking to be called by a male's name, and spent most of his first week with his hoodie up, hiding his face. He would sit visibly trembling in class, not saying a word, avoiding speech whenever possible. Two weeks in, there was still no engagement in class, still his need to get up and leave when he felt too anxious. (If you can't handle kids needing to get up whenever they feel like it, don't become a teacher.)

One evening, this student was furiously typing out what I assumed was a text. I asked him to stop, but minute later he was back at it. I stopped what I was doing again and said I would take the device from him if that would help him concentrate. He sat for a split second, then got up and went out the door. I gave the class a few last instructions,

൫

then went out to find out what was going on with him. I found him with the counselor, head down and still covered, obviously crying, at one of the tables in our lounge area.

The counselor told me that our student was feeling like he needed to talk with his former counselor from his old school right then and there and that I was not letting him. I knelt down and put my hand on his arm. Using his name, I said, "I can't help you unless you let me in." And that was all it took.

He turned a corner that night, even later shared a writing about identifying as the opposite sex in another class. He started contributing more to our discussions. I can't say there were huge grateful grins, but the hood literally came down and I could see more comfort in his eyes.

When I saw him again at his graduation, I smiled, and asked if I could give him a hug of congratulations. He agreed tentatively. Sensing his discomfort, I moved away and prayed for a smooth life ahead of him. There are times I can be naïve, but this wasn't one of them. I was all too aware this probably wasn't going to be the case, even in light of the equality movement.

ℬℭ

Chapter 37 – Those Who Can…

"Being a kid, as all kids do, you feel out of place or like kind of a freak. You wake up feeling like your head got put onto someone else's body that day."
~ John Hawkes

So do you have to be a special teacher to teach alternative Ed? Oh, yeah. What kind of teacher am I then? To be truthful, I am a lot more casual than most teachers. A fellow teacher observed me recently and even remarked she couldn't believe how relaxed I was. I don't demand silence; as I said a while ago I learned which battles to pick, and which ones to let slide. There was no point in barking at the students at Eagle as that is all they have heard their entire educational career. I heard later that I was too nice sometimes, but that is just my style. The whole "Don't smile until Christmas" thing goes against my nature, and it takes too much energy to be that mean, strict teacher. It doesn't indicate I am a slave to my kids liking me- it's simply too difficult to maintain a demeanor like that. When you are a quieter, more even-keeled teacher, when you DO get mad, let me tell you it packs a punch.

I still identify with being an alternative education teacher and probably always will as it becomes part of you, part of your inner workings.

Now that's not to say we were all other-worldly beings that had reached teaching nirvana. Every school has its weird teachers. Heck, I'm weird and I'll be the first to admit that. However, as you've met some of the folks who still call Eagle home, there were a few who may have helped perpetuate the perceived commonly-held stereotype of what an alternative education teacher is. One, of whom I am still fond, was fighting his own mental health battles, but more famously there was a very short-term one with an undisclosed drinking problem.

There was a night when this teacher did not show up for her class. First period came and went with no sign of her. My door was open and it was now second period when one of my students said to me about halfway through class, "Ooh, someone's getting fired."

I stopped and looked out into the hallway just as the office door was closing. You know it's bad when that happens.

"What did you see?" I asked as casually as I could.

"She's drunk," the student said.

"Who?"

"That other teacher," she replied.

Oh, dear. I had never seen that happen in all my years as a teacher, that one would show up to a job visibly inebriated. Yes, I had heard stories about other schools, but had never actually witnessed it. As it turned out, this teacher had somehow made it to school, and had come tottering up the steps after numerous calls from the administration searching for her. They called her husband and had him come and get her, and that was the last we saw of her.

I ran into her years later while out hiking. I wished her well, and that was it. The grapevine informed me that she ended up with a job at an online school, which was probably a much safer place for her.

The other teacher I mentioned previously was an artist and a musician, prone to writing darkly-toned poetry as he battled his own demons. It was the weekend before school and the principal had gathered us all together at a faculty member's house to start describing the new mandates regarding our teaching. All the new stuff coming down the district pipes, from writing out state requirements daily on the boards to evaluation procedures, was enough to crack this veteran teacher. Twenty-four hours to the start of the school year, he called up the principal and told him he couldn't do it anymore, that the details of what was to come was the final straw that broke the camel's back.

I didn't blame him one bit because staying ahead of all that stuff while trying to build meaningful relationships with students is just not reasonable. Nor entirely possible. I only wish politicians would figure this out, or at least think back to their school days. They might remember that it was the teachers they connected with, not the latest/greatest sparkling standard on the board that made them want to come to school in the first place.

₨ℓℂℛ

All too often, people forget teachers ARE human, and just like our students, we all come with our differences, our strengths, our weaknesses, and our quirks. Some have kids at home, some don't. Some are married, some aren't. Some are fighting illnesses; some are running marathons. Some are brand new to the profession, some are counting the days to retirement. Yes, we fall into the trap of comparing ourselves to each other, but teaching isn't a competition to be won. Money isn't the motivation, though it would be nice to be paid what we're really worth... We can dream, can't we?

It's a personal best with each and every student. Test scores and pay scales can't define a teacher's skill in what matters most in education, but a stubborn student returning to say hello can.

ഔ഑ഔ

Chapter 38 – All Aboard the Technology Train

"It has become appallingly obvious that our technology has exceeded our humanity."
~ Albert Einstein

Technology has taken over the schools and the world, sadly, but it doesn't make life a bit easier. I wouldn't be writing this book if I didn't have it.

We were excited to have computer carts coming to our school so we'd have one-to-one technology for our kids. No more "ghetto lab"! This was an awesome development. No one wanted to lose even more time hiking their class to the labs and back, so who wouldn't want these great rolling computer labs? However, they came with some drawbacks.

We tried various methods of signing the carts up, from paper to electronic calendars, but I will be the first to say NOTHING worked. We had a bad habit of snagging the carts whenever they were left unattended, too bad for anyone who was dutifully trying to use the sign out.

And as for keeping the actual cart organized? Forget it. For some reason matching the number on the computer to the slot it was supposed to go in, let alone actually hook up the charger, was like asking for a miracle. It is a statement that when kids are given everything, it's all taken for granted. They are far more likely to treat their own technology with care than what a school provides them, whether it's a "crappy Chromebook" or an iPad. On second thought, I rarely saw a kid's phone screen that wasn't spider-webbed with cracks.

Truly, nothing makes me sadder in my present-day teaching than looking around my classroom and having it look like an office. The only thing missing as kids hunch over their computers are little fabric cubicle walls and the smell of stale coffee. I could provide the standard dead plant on the windowsill with a little effort. Now there are those who believe that online schools are the wave of the future, that each teacher can easily handle a 300:1 ratio thanks to this technology. Yet study after study proves that increased screen-time leads to decreased social skills, increased depression, and lowered reading comprehension levels.

Even the mere act of handwriting is disappearing as students from kindergarten on up are encouraged to take "keyboarding" classes over learning the proper technique of holding a pencil. By the time a student reaches high school, their handwriting resembles Egyptian hieroglyphics or Sanskrit more than anything close to legible letters. Ask any teacher – we've all handed a student a paper at one point or another, asked the kid to decipher their own handwriting, and even he or she can't read it!

The abuse of technology in schools is rampant, and cyber-bullying, no matter what the programs say, is on the rise as kids find sneakier and more destructive ways to torment one another. Personally, I avoid computer use in my classrooms as much as possible because I figure these kids have the *rest of their natural lives* to sit in front of computers for their employment. Let them be kids during the time they are in school. When we had to lock the carts in middle school for months due to a kid hacking into the systems and rendering them inoperable, there were surprisingly few complaints from students OR parents.

Another thing encouraged by technology is plagiarism. It is too easy. Too tempting. And the easiest way to anger a teacher. In an early year of teaching Senior Seminar, the weekend before graduation I was grading senior papers when I found it in a student essay. A word that even I, an English major, do not use: "Whilst". If that wasn't a huge tip-off that this wasn't a student's writing, I don't know what could be. I emailed the counselor and principal, and went back to school on Monday.

That evening, the student breezed through the door, demanding his paper.

"That would be in the office with the principal, and your parents," I replied. "They are expecting you."

His face drained of all color, and he turned and left the room.

What finally resolved from this was the student had bought the paper for $7.95 off the internet and turned it in. He had to write a paper in two nights and turn it in to me to determine whether or not he would be graduating. Well, he did it, and come the night of graduation, I looked him in the eyes and asked him why he did it. He admitted he was being lazy and figuring he wouldn't get caught. The funny thing was he was a skilled writer. He hadn't had to do this to himself.

"Lesson learned, though you're out a trip to Starbucks for coffee AND a muffin," I said.

I don't know why kids think we teachers even need all the anti-plagiarism programs out there. We get to know them through their writing. We know when it is their own, and when it isn't. What words they tend to use, and what words they don't. We know how students structure a sentence, and can easily spot which sentences there is no way in heck that kid wrote. It's really not that hard.

Credit where credit is due, kids. Simple as that.

ℬℭ

Chapter 39 – Things Got a Little Dramatic Literature

"It's got to do with putting yourself in other people's shoes and seeing how far you can come to truly understand them. I like the empathy that comes from acting."
~ Christian Bale

My Dramatic Literature class had the benefit of having some former drama students in it one quarter a few years ago. They were your typical drama kids – as in always creating drama. However, they were fairly harmless. We were reading the documentary novel <u>Nothing but the Truth</u> by Avi, a middle school-level reading book, but written in almost a play format, so it begged to be interpreted. There were no directions for the "actors", nor set descriptions; only times. There was much to be left to the imagination, and this is exactly what my students did.

One evening, my two drama boys decided to play the part of the mother and father in a scene where the couple was bickering over dinner about their son's suspension. One of the students decided the part of the mother should be played as an affected Scottish woman, while the father character was determined to bellow every word so it could be heard clearly through the wall to the next classroom. Needless to say, much of the scene's wording was lost when the Scottish "mom" fell into improvising her under-appreciated efforts from slaving over the stove all day, and the father continued to try to project his voice across the street. How these students kept a straight face I will never know because the rest of us had completely dissolved.

This same group completed all the requisite texts early enough in the quarter that for once we had time to spare. They opted to find a play we could actually perform in front of the rest of the school. Well, performing is a strong word – it was more like Reader's Theater as there was no way we had time to memorize all of those lines. The formerly Scottish Woman actor found an Australian play that I okayed. And I should have read more closely. There was a line in there that would make anyone blush, and as I had to read that part that night, there will be no forgetting it in this lifetime. Once more the class was reduced to fits, and admittedly I was, too. I mean I know there are teacher-y times when I am supposed to get upset over the inappropriate, but there are other times when it is so unexpected it's too late to get serious and you just have to laugh about it.

We went on to do a Reader's Theater reading of the play to the school one night before graduation, even scoring the auditorium for our "performance". As it happens the last week before graduation, the seniors don't have to attend if their grades are strong enough. Naturally, my lead actress, who had promised she would come that night to do her part, didn't appear. That left me to have to read her part.

I must admit my biggest regret in high school was not taking Drama. I think I could have been pretty good at it. I've never been afraid of the stage since a fifth grade rendition of "Short People" by Al Newman, so I was up for the challenge.

The best part was I was able to one-up the Scottish Woman because the line directed at him was to get to call him a "little sh*t" in front of the entire school. Ah, sweet revenge. From that night on my students suggested I should have had to do push-ups for that indiscretion. With a smirk, I simply claimed, "I was reading my line."

In Their Own Words:

How I came to arrive at Eagle Academy is I was lost in school, I felt like there was no option and that I needed to drop out for my own happiness. I was having a large amount of problems with bullying. I was troubled with emotions flying back and forth and finally I just couldn't take it anymore, then my principal from Ponderosa High School told me about eagle academy which was going to be my last shot at anything high school related.

When I got to the school, my world changed. I was transformed from the kid that would sit in the corner and not talk, to striving to be just as good as the teachers that taught me. My impressions of the teachers? In my book, they are family. They showed me not only the way to learn but they also showed me how to bring out my personality and live my life. Those teachers are some of the world's best and that school was by far the best thing for me.

The students? They weren't just students either, they are family as well, the amount of comradery that is in that school is best described as better school spirit than High School Musical. The students also showed me no matter where you are from or what you have done you will always fit in with them. We used to play hacky-sack in the hall way and the teachers I could greet and have a smile on my face. From what I saw, the students always came out of their shells and became themselves. What am I doing now? Well, simply put I'm following my dream. If there is one thing I learned from that school, it's that don't ever be scared to follow your dreams and not to let anyone tell you that you cannot achieve it. So, shortly after graduating I joined the United States Marine Corps and am currently an Analyst stationed in Beaufort, South Carolina. I took everything I learned from that school and used it as my foundation to build my life and be what I always wanted to be so one day I could "Stand in the Hall of Fame".

~Matt Dillon

ℰℭ

Spring Class of 2010

Chapter 40 - A Return to Arms

"It's no use going back to yesterday, because I was a different person then."
~ Lewis Carroll, Alice in Wonderland

Returning to Eagle to visit has been strange. So many new faces on the staff, a different schedule for the evening classes, but some of my former kids remained. It occurred to me that within another semester, I would no longer recognize any students, and the thought made me sad.

For that reason, I attended the winter 2016 graduation to see a few of my formers cross that stage. I found a staff member sitting in the hall practicing his congratulations speech and asked him to sneak me back to the "green room" so I could see the graduates I knew before the ceremony. I knew I would get lost in the final hubbub afterwards, not just due to my height, but I was being selfish and wanted them to myself for a few minutes before the families took over.

When I walked in, I was immediately tackle-hugged by the same student who, weeks before during a visit, I had to ask put me down from one of his bear hugs. He looked great on his cap and gown, and we took a few selfies to commemorate the occasion. I visited with the girl who had burst into tears at my last visit, one of the unbelievably quiet boys I had, and with our transgender student who had done his best to stay invisible when he first arrived at the school. It appeared he had begun his hormone therapy changes as there were whiskers on his chin, and he looked like he was standing up a little taller. Eye contact was still kept to a minimum.

A few more kids found me in the crowd and there were hugs all around. I watched them take their final group photo, a little sad that this was no longer a task I would take on, that being making sure that photo and the list of names go into the local paper. Someone else was going to have to do that now.

Earlier I spotted the principal and went to give an awkward hello hug. He said he'd like to give a recognition to me, and I said I'd be honored.

The call was raised for the students to begin lining up for the march into the auditorium. The counselor had emailed to tell me he'd save a seat for me in the front row, so I made my way down. The entire front row was reserved as it always was, so I sat down and said hello to the people behind me. Turned out that their daughter was graduating tonight- I had only glanced at the list of names- and sitting with them was the brother I had as a student who did not make it due to attendance issues. He looked up awkwardly from a row behind them and told me all was well, that he had opted to get his GED. "Good for you," I said. At least he had chosen not to remain a dropout.

I took a moment to scan the audience and spotted a few former students, one who had one night, after making a huge life mistake, sat on the floor sobbing in my arms. That soft spot in my heart went out to him once more, and I was hoping to see him after the ceremony to check on him, but he had disappeared by that time.

Quite shocking to me was the entrance of the board members, among them, for the first time in the decade I'd been there, an actual superintendent was in attendance. We had had the assistant superintendent on occasion before, then some titled representatives, but never the actual super. And especially that one. I couldn't help smirk as it had become clear as of late, since the latest election was tipping things back in the direction of people who cared about kids and not privatization, she was doing her level best to come off as caring. Smiling next to her was one of the newest board members, one I actively supported. The juxtaposition was pronounced.

The ceremony started and I stood, my old reflexes kicking in as the staff walked in. Doc squeezed my shoulder affectionately as she walked past. I couldn't help but notice that there were so few of them, taking up only a quarter of the front row when we used to take up nearly the whole thing. Then the graduates came in and the Curmudgeon indicated the crowd should stand. The procession moved up the stairs and down, cameras clicking and cheers from all parts of the audience, the always-stirring "Pomp and Circumstance " playing as they took the stage.
As the ceremony began, so did the live streaming, and true to his word, the principal called my name in the introduction of former students and staff. Sadly, I was the only returning staff member as the other nine who had been dismissed weren't in attendance. I didn't really blame them for any hard feelings.

Student after student had their picture and future plans shown over the stage as they said their personal two minutes. Two boys burst into grateful tears before their speeches were completed, telling their parents they would make them proud. And pretty much reduced everyone in the audience to weepy applause.

At the end of the commencement, kids and families gathered in the lobby area for pictures and hugs, and the staff moved among the groups to congratulate the now-former students individually. It was bittersweet, knowing that this was probably my second to last ceremony before I would no longer know the kids. I hugged the few I knew that had not yet moved off to celebrate, met a few parents, and talked with some staff.

The staff Curmudgeon said he missed having me around, although I can't be 100% sure he said it just that way.

I found the principal and thanked him for the nod, and while he invited me to go out afterwards, as was tradition for the staff, I felt uncomfortable, like I had already overstayed my welcome. The newer staff deserved their time with each other, and I already felt like the reactions some of the kids gave me before the ceremony may have been hard for this staff to understand. Yeah, that sounds a bit egotistical, but I am a pretty good study of human behavior. If I wasn't, I wouldn't be a teacher.

In Their Own Words:

So... My Eagle Academy experience! My parents thought I needed a change in environment, so they moved my sister and I to Highlands Ranch. I was attending Highlands Ranch High, while my sister was going to Eagle Academy. We would compare schools and some of the things she would tell me about Eagle sounded too good to be true, so I asked for a transfer.

My first afternoon with Eagle Academy I knew I was in the right place. For starters, the staff was great, friendly, professional, and each staff member had a great sense of humor in their own way. Makes things a lot easier when having conversation about absences, tardiness and behavioral issues.

Scheduling was fantastic! I worked from 6:30AM to 2:30 PM, and school at 3:15pm. I was working full time, and had time to get home, change, eat, wash my car etc. Most of the time I'd stay in my work clothes because, well... Why not. A majority of students do not have full time jobs, so going to school in a work uniform was bragging rights in my eyes.

Which brings me to my next point, Eagle had a relaxed dress code! Wearing baseball caps, and jerseys were permitted. You cannot find that at a normal school.

Speaking of a normal school, classroom sizes at Eagle were about half the size, maybe even less, than a normal high school class.

Advantages of having smaller classes: shy students don't get stomach jitters when having to speak in front of an audience, teachers can have one on one time with students that are falling behind, you know everyone at school, which leads to a friendly environment. No social boundaries or cliques that keep to themselves like a normal school...

I loved sports; unfortunately, Eagle did not have an athletic program. Instead we had a work program, which teaches you the value of working full time, and the responsibility that comes with having bills. Which I believe was a greater message. "Preparation for adulthood" is what I would call it.

On a last note, I really like to point out, every school I've attended, the relationship I had with staff members was business only. At Eagle I had more of a friendship with each and every staff member, [which] made the rest of my high school days much smoother, and also very very emotional when it was time to part ways. In a nutshell Eagle Academy staff was the foundation of my success and completing the high school chapter of life.

~Victor Conoway

℅℃

Chapter 41 – The Man, The Myth, The Legend

"In every case where I've seen a transformational school, there's a principal who really has the foundational experience of having taught successfully."
~ Wendy Kopp

None other than THE Doug Seligman, former principal of Eagle Academy, was made aware I was writing this book, and suggested we get together for lunch. He was the heart and soul of Eagle during the eight years we served there together, and my respect for him ran deep. So deep, in fact, that when he expressed interest in discussing my project I grew a little worried I was about to get "schooled". The man's effect on people was profound.

We met at a little Greek restaurant outside of the University of Denver campus. The weather was one of those unusually warm February days when residents of the state would have chosen to sit outside in shirtsleeves were it not gale-force, early Spring winds. He was already seated when I walked in, busy with some electronic device. But for the next two hours the conversation was non-stop. Catching up on students, reliving stories from "the good old days", and me asking questions about him I never knew the answers to, and that I needed answers to for my own edification. Most specifically, how do people end up in Alternative Education?

Often in the teaching profession, teachers arrive at their career because of his or her personal experience in education, and/or a special teacher inspired them. As was my case. Thank you, Mrs. Corbin, for being my English teacher my Sophomore year and setting me on my path.

Other teachers told me they were "special education" kid, or an alternative education kid, and they wanted to "pay it forward" so to speak. Me? Not even close. Gifted/Talented kid who went to private school, skipped second grade, repeated Junior year, and headed out into the world with a college trust fund. I "fell" into alternative education by answering that job posting for a long-term substitute, and I fell madly in love with the feel that what I was doing was oh-so-much more than education.

Back to our lunch, Doug asked me what had happened the last two years I was there and I had to be truthful. It just wasn't the same place anymore. The stricter rules, the less-than-welcome feeling former students would get when returning for a visit. The new principal was turning it into HIS school, which was of course natural, but it was hard for Doug to hear. He even remarked at one point, "It's upsetting to know that everything we all built and worked for is gone, and I suppose that was my fault."

I said it absolutely wasn't, that all things change and it was a phenomenal place back when he was at the helm. He left a legacy that will never be erased. And I guess that is the lesson, that as painful as change is, going back is never an option. You just keep moving forward.

Here is Doug in his own words:

1. How did you end up in alternative education? Did you study a specific path to get there?

I am not certain that a specific path exists to get into Alt-Ed. That particular population selects the teacher. I conducted my administrative internship at Eagle Academy back in 2001, so I was familiar with what the work of the school was when I applied for the open position in 2002, even though I didn't get it that time, though it worked out that I was able to stay with my seminar students at TRHS and read their names on stage at Red Rocks for graduation! What I figured out upon taking the job in 2004 was that Alt-Ed is often the forgotten child at the feast. Regular Ed folks can attend training and workshops, but there was very, very little for folks like us. That is primarily why Becca M. I set up the first Alternative Education Conference in my second year to see what other leaders were doing. Then I discovered the National Alternative Education Association and attended their national conference four different times. I also served, for a year, on the communications committee as a volunteer.

৪৩৫৫

2. What was your personal background as a student?

Totally a fixed mindset kind of kid. I was an early reader, so that put me into upper reading groups at a very young age which led me to believe that I was smarter than most other kids. This caught up to me when I was in high school because whereas I did have the capacity for learning, I did not have the endurance to push myself when the work grew more difficult. I cruised through high school with less than great grades until I was a senior, having moved to a part of the country I didn't particularly enjoy or wished to remain, so self-motivation showed up, I earned A's and B's, and moved out of state to go to college. Even there, I majored mostly in building a social life while at UNM. Eventually, I dropped out to enlist in the US Army to find myself, and, boy, did I ever. My pre-enlistment scores on the ASVAB and the DLAB suggested that I might be facile with languages, something that I would never have guessed in my high school Spanish classes. I ended up at the Defense Language Institute studying Czech in a 47-week immersion course and learned intimately what being a struggling student feels like. I stayed at the bottom of my class until about ten minutes before our final exams when I felt the clouds part and the ability to speak, read, and write in a second language become second nature to me. Easily the hardest educational adventure I have ever undertaken.

3. What was your favorite moment at Eagle?

Too many to recount, honestly. I would say that one of my proudest moments came while accompanying a trio of students to the NAEA conference in Atlanta my final year at Eagle. Their teacher was no longer with us, but flights and reservations had been made, so we flew out to make a presentation without any visuals or scripts. The team sat down to plan who would create the slide show, who would speak at what time, and, after a little practice, they did so and not only pulled it off, but were also informed by the adult educators in the room that they had never participated in such a professional and authentic presentation.

4. What was your most trying moment at Eagle?

ℰℭ

We endured that deaths of two parents during my nine years at Eagle, and even though we rallied everyone around those students to provide support and assistance, the initial experiences were tough. And I hated having to put students on a leave of absence for failing to pass their Student Success Scores, but I also knew that it was a learning opportunity that had to be provided.

5. What was the biggest lesson you learned in the alternative education environment?

Students will only listen to teachers if they feel they are heard as well. Our motto of "Accept, then Expect" reminds us of that. If we take kids where they are academically and offer them a safe and nurturing environment, they will grow and thrive. And not all alternative schools are the same. Many of them provide strong curricular options which allow students to move into the same post-secondary options as their former peers in the general education world.

6. If someone were going to go into alternative education, what advice would you give him or her?

Avoid Alt-Ed if you lack flexibility and need to be right all of the time. Working in the Alt-Ed world is similar to working in nature. No one can possibly survive by pushing back against the elements. It is by understanding when to stand and when to bend that a person can not only survive but also succeed.

7. What kinds of people made for good staff members? How did you know he or she was a good fit? Or a not-so-good fit?

Good staff members come up with ways to reach what can be a highly resistant group of students. Great staff members help students take a role in their own education and see that there is a tangible goal past graduation. Poor staff are rigid and right.

ၰၨ

After lunch, blissfully full of Greek food and good conversation.

Spring Class of 2014

In Their Own Words:

I did four years of traditional high school and did not graduate. Once I was told I would not be graduating, I was told that the "best thing for me" would be to study for the GED and take the test. My then best friend, Kim was attending Eagle at the time and kept telling me how much she enjoyed it. I continued to work and study for the GED for close to another month until Kim talked to me about Eagle again. This time I had taken of the the tests and failed. Kim was finally able to talk me into meeting her for dinner at the school one night. I met her inside and as I was waiting for her, [I met] the man who truly made me fall in love with learning, [there] was the principal, Mr. Seligman!! He remembered who I was from four years prior. We made small talk and told him how I was unable to graduate from my traditional school. As I told him what was going on, tears filled my eyes. He brought me into his office to fill out an application to the school. He explained to me that there was only one spot left and he had given it to me!! He believed in me when I could no longer believe in myself. This is how I started the path to the rest of my life!! The smallest action from one man truly paved the way to my future!

I started that next Monday. I was given my class schedule and a counselor. Mrs. Bliek was my rock for the year that I was at the school. I was going through a lot at home. She was nothing but supportive of me and my decisions, no matter what. I was never judged by her. There were a few nights where I would sit in her office and just cry for hours. Somehow, at the end of the night, she made me feel better and that reassured me that everything would be okay.

Once I started going to class and getting to know my teachers, one really made an impact on me and my education, Mrs. K!! She showed me that I was a person and not just a student. She reminded me of how great I was. She showed me that I was smart and a great person. She even reminded me of how much I loved to write.

Here we are, 10 years later. These four key people are still in my life. They still show me that I am a wonderful person and that I can do anything I put my mind to. I am a single mother of one. I proudly work for an asphalt and concrete company and strive to be the best I can be. I plan to move up in the company and grow here. I am starting college fall of 2017. None of this would be possible without these 4 people who believed in me when I didn't think there was anything to believe in!!
~Dominique DeBello

Winter Class of 2012

Chapter 42 -Turn On, Tune In, Drop-Out?

"Sometimes you just gotta be drop-kicked out of the nest."
~ Robert Downey, Jr.

Timothy Leary in 1966 San Francisco offered this infamous life mantra: "Turn on' meant go within to activate your neural and genetic equipment. Become sensitive to the many and various levels of consciousness and the specific triggers that engage them. Drugs were one way to accomplish this end. 'Tune in"' meant interact harmoniously with the world around you - externalize, materialize, express your new internal perspectives. 'Drop out' suggested an active, selective, graceful process of detachment from involuntary or unconscious commitments. 'Drop Out' meant self-reliance, a discovery of one's singularity, a commitment to mobility, choice, and change. Unhappily my explanations of this sequence of personal development were often misinterpreted to mean 'Get stoned and abandon all constructive activity'."

Well, yeah. But what I'm referring to is the notion of dropping out of high school and pursuing a GED (General Equivalency Diploma). There were many a student who threatened to do just that, even some who made this determination with mere weeks to go until their graduation. It was baffling. Was it a signal that this student needed something even more than we could give? Or just a testing of how much we would beg them to stay? Whatever the reason, we would do just that, telling them that a GED, while preferable to dropping out altogether, still carries a stigma in the business community. Some readers here may deny that, but a GED often indicates the earner is not a team player, that they would choose to work on their own over learning to get along, or overcome obstacles in the field of socializing with other human beings. Granted some people do not have the luxury to choose the path upon which they are set, but when you are two weeks away from graduating?! Come on!

So we kicked some student tail when it came to such decisions. I used to say, "I'll love you across the finish line, or kick you across, but that's your only choice." Surely someone somewhere will get the impression that it's not okay to say these kinds of things to students lest the words are misinterpreted, but this was the way some of these kids needed to be talked to. No one else in his or her immediate surroundings would. And you know what? They loved us for it.

In Their Own Words:

I came to Eagle when I ran out of other options. The people in regular high school bullied me, and I was seen as an outcast among my peers. I began failing my classes because I never showed up. I was afraid of eating in the lunch room at a table by myself. I was scared of the words that my peers called me behind my back. I then became a failure in the eyes of my parents and the school system. I was told that I should just drop out and get my GED because I was wasting everyone's time. That irritated me. It irritated me knowing that people thought so little of me without actually trying to understand me or my struggles. It irritated me that someone could look me in the face and tell me that I was a waste of space because I didn't meet the requirements of their conformity.

I had completely lost my support system by the end of my Freshman year. My parents had given up; I was too difficult of a child for them to deal with. My counselors didn't know what to do with me anymore, either. It was me against the world, and I was okay with that. Halfway through my junior year, I realized that I was not a failure. I decided that I wanted to better myself, that I wanted to succeed. I realized that I wasn't going to be able to succeed in regular high school, so I left and tried a couple of other options. I eventually found my way to Eagle Academy. I came to the school with 24 missing credits and very tough skin. I was very cold and distant with my teachers and peers for the first week. I expected them to be exactly like all of the other teachers and classmates I encountered at my other schools. I wanted them to know that I was only here to graduate, and nothing else. I didn't want to make friends; I didn't want to talk to any of my peers. I didn't care about anyone else's opinion anymore, and I was used to being alone.

After the first week, and about 100 Facebook friend requests from fellow classmates, I began to warm up to the school. My teachers took a vested interest in me, which was a new experience for me. I wasn't used to someone in my academic career caring about me. It felt amazing to know that I wasn't alone anymore. My teachers cared about how well I did in their classes, and about what was going on in my life. Eagle was like one giant family. We all protected each other and we all cared for each other. Everyone at that school, including the students, lifted each other up. The environment of this school was refreshing. It allowed me to do my best and be my best. The teachers set great examples for the students, and the students looked to each other for support. I worked my butt off at this school because I finally had the support to drive me to do so. I graduated from this school in June of 2015, on time and with the best grades I had ever gotten in my academic career. This school gave me everything that I needed to prove the people that doubted me wrong. I am now excelling in college, and I am on my way to getting my RN in nursing. I have this school, the teachers, and my fellow classmates to thank for my incredible success.

I will never forget the moment that my school principal told me that my teachers had nominated me to give one of three speeches at my graduation. I would have never gotten that opportunity at my old high school. I will never forget walking up onto that stage, all eyes on me, and overcoming my fear of talking in front of that many people. I will never forget the feeling that all of those people clapping at the end of my speech gave me. I will never forget the moment one of teachers had to put sunglasses on in the middle of my speech so that I wouldn't be able to see him cry. I will never forget the opportunities that this school gave me. I will never forget the day that I came into my math class bawling my eyes out because I was just told that I wouldn't be able to talk to my father for a while, and my math teacher told me that I could write instead of completing the assignment. I wrote the best story I have ever written that day, and it was because my teacher was more concerned about my well-being than about the assignment. I will never forget the love that I felt in my English class, my mythology class, my math class, my economic class, and my sci-fi class. I will never forget the support that I had at this school. I will never forget the teachers of this school and everything that they have done for me. I will never forget the new found hope that this school instilled in me. This school was a gift, and I'm glad I ended up here. I'm not so sure that I would have gotten this far in my life without the people and the teachers at this school.

~Kelsi Campanella

෩ඕ

<u>Chapter 43 - A Pregnant Pause</u>

"If we as a nation are to break the cycle of poverty, crime and the growing underclass of young people ill equipped to be productive citizens, we need to not only implement effective programs to prevent teen pregnancy, but we must also help those who have already given birth so that they become effective, nurturing, bonding parents."
~ Jane Fonda

Teaching is a multi-generational adventure as many more seasoned teachers than I can attest. I have seen many of my students grow up and get married, get jobs and have families, not necessarily always in that order.

Many an Eagle student had babies outside of getting married, and often times that made me and a few other staff members quite sad. The reason being we all knew the struggles they would face being a young single parent while trying to finish school and get a job to support them both. I'm sure any one of them would tell you in retrospect that it was indeed difficult, but that they wouldn't have done anything different. While that is the standard answer of anyone who became a parent before they were even remotely settled in life, I would venture a guess some of them would, at least momentarily, chosen to have had a different outcome if they could have gone back in time. I can only say this with the disclaimer that I knew how panicked I was when late monthlies had me worried I was pregnant before I was even 20 years old.

So alternative education kids, and regular ed kids too, for that matter, still do get pregnant out of wedlock. I know this isn't such a big deal anymore, but when you teach in an alt-ed environment and everyone is talking about how wonderful it is the teen pregnancy rate has gone down, you look around and shake your head a little. It still happens, and even though you are dismayed, it's nothing compared to what their parents go through, and what struggles you know this young person is going to face. What you do then is double your efforts to at least make sure they finish high school and get a diploma. Bring the baby to class if you have to, you tell them. But make for darn sure they don't stop coming as you know a high school diploma may be the only certificate they get for a while as they raise a baby without a desirable amount of support.

As they raise a baby while all of their friends are talking about the show coming up that weekend, the young parent knows they will most likely not get to go. The young mother or father listens in class to their friends talking about getting together after class, but they know they need to go pick up the baby from the sitter's house. You, the teacher, just have to stand back and watch, much like a parent, and keep your mouth closed as much as you can.

I slipped one night in a casual discussion, angry at the mentality that a young parent could do it all on their own to begin with. Forgetting myself, I blurted, "Girls, just keep your legs closed!" Not one of my finer, sensitive teacher moments. The one young mother in my class that I had forgotten was a parent said, "In my defense, I had had a lot to drink that night!"

Crap. Oops. Every other thought you think when you stick your foot in your mouth.

What this young mom was not ready to acknowledge at the time, and I did not know, was the fact she was, by every definition of a woman being taken advantage of, raped that night and became pregnant. Only a few months later, during a presentation from another day high school drama program about date rape did I see this young mom get up from the assembly with another girl and hurriedly leave the room.

Pregnancy happens in teens still. We who are older and (most of the time) wiser know what troubles they face in their futures; just be sure the older, wiser part of you keeps his or her mouth closed in the education environment, and you do everything possible to get them to cross that stage for their diploma. The night the young parent I have been speaking of received her high school diploma, her toddler called out from the audience, "I love you, mommy!"

In this case, her child became her driving force. And I am happy to report the story has a happy ending as I know this young adult is now a practicing nurse.

ෂංෂ

Winter Class of 2009

ℬᎤᏓ

Chapter 44 -Monkey See, Monkey Do

"This much I have learned: human beings come with very different sets of wiring, different interests, different temperaments, different learning styles, different gifts, different temptations. These differences are tremendously important in the spiritual formation of human beings."
~ John Ortberg

Kinesthetic learners are the people who learn by doing. They need physical motion and feedback in order to process a skill. For example, learning a golf swing cannot be done by listening to a lecture about it; one has to practice the swing to commit it to muscle memory. Most humans learn this way, but look what we do to younger humans in traditional school settings - force them to sit in desks, virtually motionless save being hunched over a computer. These kinds of students need physical sensation in order to learn.

Looking around an Eagle classroom, one would notice multiple piercings, tattoos, large gauges in earlobes, and constant movement when confined to a chair. It all fit. The majority of these students must be kinesthetic learners in need of physical stimulation, otherwise why the prevalence of body modification? Kinesthetic Learners have to *feel* something, some stimulus, in order to learn. If you looked around my class circle, something on every student was moving – pen tapping, foot jiggling, or some practicing their latest dance club finger-moves for their LED gloves. (This really is a thing, too.) My thoughts, or "wonderings" if you insist on another ridiculous pop-education term, was that this was also the reason these kids had multiple tattoos and piercings, frequently dyed their hair, and often, more sinisterly, practiced self-mutilation such as cutting.

Testing my theory on this concept, I had many of my classes moving. We did ropes course activities in the hall, changed location of classes, sat on the floor. The kids were more engaged in what is traditionally not the most exciting, nor the most active of subjects.

English Language Arts is simply a more cerebral subject. There are only so many adjective raps or verb charades a student can create in their schooling career before it comes down to the somewhat arduous-to-them task of reading. I learned to look around for student investment in a lesson, and when I recognized it was flagging, I would quickly suggest a move to the floor. The kids were always compliant in this request, male or female. It was the physical feedback on more pressure points in the body receiving input, as any biofeedback expert would confirm.

This isn't groundbreaking news, but the obvious recommendation for an alternative education classroom would be to ditch the desks, if possible, and replace them with all sorts of different styles of seats. The exercise balls idea common for younger grade levels would be a disaster in the making. Trust me; there was an exercise ball in my classroom for a day student, but it only provided being endlessly amusing as my kids kicked it back and forth in the middle of our class circle. I let them, of course, because it amused me too. But I'm also a kinesthetic learner. And yes, I have multiple ear-piercings and two tattoos. I never asked the other teachers about their body modifications if they weren't already visible, but I assumed we were all there, staff and student alike, because something about it appealed to all of us.

Perhaps it was the more intimate "feel" of the smaller class sizes. One can't really hide in the back. You can't escape connecting with people.

Perhaps it was the oft-studied, but seldom accommodated by schools, circadian rhythms of teenagers allowing them in be more alert in the evenings that inspired the adults. (Teens are naturally more active after 11:00 am to nearly 12:00 am.) It's hard to say, but I am sticking to my theory that an alternative education campus is a kinesthetic learner magnet.

Check with psychologist Howard Gardener on the other six learning styles if you are so inclined; although, he, himself, said at one point there was a little too much enthusiasm for his Seven Multiple Intelligences theory.

But you want answers to the question *How?* I know. This should help – it's the last part of the table for At-Risk Twice-Exceptional Kids presented in the beginning of the book:

School Support	Home Support
Don't lower expectations	Seek counseling for family
Diagnostic testing	Avoid power struggles
Non-traditional study skills	Involvement in extracurricular activities
In-depth studies and mentorship	Assess for dangerous behavior
G.E.D.	Keep dialogue open
Academic coaching	Hold accountable
Home visits	Minimize punishments
Promote resilience	Communicate confidence in ability to
Discuss secondary options	overcome obstacles
Aggressive advocacy	Preserve relationships

Figure B: Maureen Neihart and George Betts, 2010

Check, check, and check at Eagle. I would strongly encourage, however, further specialized training for educators, advice I am taking myself. And parents, please look into available counseling classes if you feel your own child has been described at all in this book.

Notice students all on the floor during Creative Writing. We were sharing "campfire" ghost stories, and the student with his head down recalled doing a similar task with his seventh grade teacher, a friend of mine, and using a cell phone flashlight to illuminate crumpled colored paper for a "fire".

Winter Class of 2013

In Their Own Words:

There are moments in time that you just know will unequivocally change the course of your life forever. It sounds extreme, but graduating from Eagle Academy was one of those moments for me. You see, it was more than just graduating and receiving a piece of paper that said I had completed the state mandated four years of high school. There was a time that I thought my life choices had steered me down a path of mediocrity and hardship. Eagle gave me a second chance to make better choices and chose a different path; a better path.

I started high school at a private all-girls school my parents had worked hard to get me into. They only wanted what was best for me. A higher education led to a better college, a better job, and a better life. I did my best to fit in and be a 'normal' teenager. I was always a tomboy but I started wearing make-up, did my hair, went to homecoming, and joined the volleyball team. Unfortunately, my personal life was in shambles and I struggled to keep the chaos at home from affecting my studies. I sought comfort in drugs, drinking, sex and it was only a matter of time before my choices caught up to me. At the beginning of my junior year, I found out I was pregnant. I felt like my entire world was crashing in. Despite my fears, I decided to keep the baby and when I told my school, they suggested that I withdraw. Surely, a sixteen-year-old could never keep up with her studies and raise a baby.

Within a month of dropping out, I was no longer welcomed at my mother's house and I moved in with the father of the child I was carrying. I had never felt more lost in my entire life. I wasn't in school; I was barely on speaking terms with my parents, and was desperately trying to make my relationship work with the father of my child, despite his struggles with a serious drug problem. I remember a nurse telling me at one of my appointments that a majority of young mothers never graduate high school, have another child within the first two years, and end up on welfare for the rest of their lives. I refused to be another statistic.

I finished my junior year by homeschooling myself and attending a small alternative school one day a week. I walked those halls, seven months pregnant, and tried to ignore all the stares and judgmental comments that were directed towards me, my giant belly, and empty ring finger. I was determined to make my senior year different. Quitting and getting a GED wasn't good enough. Somehow, what the nurse said stuck with me and pushed me to strive for more.

I don't remember how I found Eagle Academy, but I do remember pulling into the parking lot one August afternoon, pulling my newborn baby out of the car, and walking up the steps to the administration office. Somehow I knew this was my only chance to graduate and that's exactly what I told the principal when I sat down across from him that day. I remember almost begging him to let me go there. I had to graduate. I had to prove everyone wrong. I left Eagle that day with a small glimpse of hope. I had been accepted and would start in just a few weeks. At that time my only goal was to go there, study hard, and get my diploma. I had no idea what an impact Eagle and the people inside those walls would have on me.

Eagle became a second family to me, something I had no idea I needed so badly. I became close with the other students because I felt little to no judgment. There were other teen moms there who understood the struggle that came with having a child so young. I became even closer to the teachers, who accepted me and my daughter like their own. I was able to bring my daughter with me when times were rough or daycare fell through. I learned to stand up for myself and my friends when before, I was afraid to speak my mind. I met one of my best friends in my English class at Eagle. She stood by me five years later as I married the love of my life and was right by my side again when I had my second child. I graduated Eagle with more than just a diploma. I graduated with life-long friendships with both teachers and staff. I graduated with a sense of worth. I proved I was more than just another teen mom statistic.

Since graduating, I was able to leave a very toxic, dangerous relationship with the father of my first child. I learned to value myself and reject anyone who couldn't do the same. I settled down and married someone who loves me and my daughter as his own. I continued on to college and received my Associates degree and am still working on my Bachelors. I still keep up with several of my teachers from Eagle, as well as many students that I've formed a bond with. We will always have something in common. We all struggled, we all came from different backgrounds, and we all found Eagle.
~Halle Althoff

ഇൻരു

<u>Chapter 45 -The Last Chapter.</u>

"A Teacher opens the door. You walk through by yourself."
~Chinese proverb

In the final few scenes from the movie *Fast Times at Ridgemont High*, beleaguered teacher Mr. Hand gets his revenge on student Jeff Spicoli on the pinnacle of high school, Prom Night. After all the time Spicoli wasted in Mr. Hand's class, Mr. Hand determines he gets to waste about three hours of Spicoli's time, effectively keeping him from attending Prom.

The camera pans a dimly lit, obviously male-inhabited bedroom, replete with Playboy foldouts and surfer paraphernalia. No doubt the fragrance in there is pungent.

The two end up having a political conversation in surfer-speak about the colonists trying to avoid being "bogus" like Mother England, and Mr. Hand concludes that this response is "close". Viewers can tell that the teacher has to concede that, while not the traditional answer he was looking for, for this particular student the understanding he at last demonstrated was suitable to meet the needs of a history lesson. The symbolism of Mr. Hand being in Spicoli's domain for this reflects a teacher's greatest method, and that is meeting a student where they are at. Bad grammar notwithstanding, this is what educators, all over America at least, are told: "Meet them where they're at." And so he does. And so we do, but in no purer form than we did at Eagle.

Back to the movie, Spicoli, in a moment of genuine interest, asks Mr. Hand if there is a student Mr. Hand makes an example of every year, much like himself. Mr. Hand doesn't answer directly, choosing instead to suggest Spicoli may be repeating a year and will find out himself.

The student panics, begging to know, "What? You're going to flunk me?"

Mr. Hand then assures Spicoli he may "squeak by" his class, and the two shake hands. They reached a mutual point of respect when Mr.

Hand used one last ploy to get through to the student and evened up the score.

"Aloha, Mr. Hand," Spicoli smiles.

"Aloha, Jeff," Mr. Hand states, and he leaves Spicoli's life.

I think this example from the movie is only fitting as a representation of what goes on in alternative education environments, as well as more than a few other schools. Spicoli spends the entire movie fighting Mr. Hand and usurping his authority, while Mr. Hand's only desire is to educate youths and make them know his or her place in the grand puzzle of life. His magnum opus is this devil-may-care, infuriating example.

Then only in the end, in Mr. Hand's last attempt to influence Spicoli in a positive fashion, does the student learn to respect the "master" and everything the man has been trying to teach. And he doesn't hate Mr. Hand for it. On the contrary, the student offers his hand first to the teacher as their "wasted" (not that way) evening comes to an end, illustrating that the student's walls have finally cracked enough to let in a little ray of humanity. Both characters arrive at their conclusions: the authority figure is not such a despot after all, and every student is valuable, no matter how aggravating.

I am reminded ultimately of a saying that reads, "When the student is ready, the teacher will appear." Sometimes, just sometimes, those teachers are a little harder to find, and they don't fit the mold, just the way some students don't. But they are still there, waiting to open the doors no matter what time of day.

www.ingramcontent.com/pod-product-compliance
Lightning Source LLC
LaVergne TN
LVHW091217080426
835509LV00009B/1047